David BECKHAM

portrait of a superstar

What do you see when you think of David Beckham?

For many people it is one half of the most talked and written about couple in the country.

There's a fascination about his tattoos, his cars, and virtually every item of clothing he wears off the football pitch.

But while all that is undoubtedly part of the David Beckham phenomenon, they are all merely sideshows, distractions from the substance...the *real* David Beckham.

David BECKHAM

portrait of a superstar

Fergus Kelly

■SCHOLASTIC

Scholastic Children's Books
Commonwealth House, 1-19 New Oxford Street
London WC1A 1NU
a division of Scholastic Ltd

London ~ New York ~ Toronto ~ Sydney ~ Auckland
Mexico City ~ New Delhi ~ Hong Kong

First published in the UK by Scholastic Ltd, 2001

Text copyright © Fergus Kelly, 2001

ISBN 0 439 98173 5

Printed by Cox & Wyman Ltd, Reading, Berks

The publishers would like to thank the following sources for their kind
permission to reproduce the pictures in this book:

Front Cover: Pic © London Features International (front)

Colour insert: Pg 1: PA Photos / Dave Kendall; Pg 2: PA Photos / Sean Dempsey (top);
Pg 3: Pic © London Features International; Pg 4: Pic © London Features International;
Pg 5: PA Photos / John Stillwell; Pg 6: PA Photos / David Jones.

2 4 6 8 10 9 7 5 3 1

For Emily Ward

contents

chapter ONE
off   9

chapter TWO
chase lane dreamer   14

chapter THREE
a ticket to the theatre   21

chapter FOUR
away from home   27

chapter FIVE
physical education   37

chapter SIX
even Pele never did that   47

chapter SEVEN
a question of focus   57

chapter EIGHT
'one stupid boy'   68

chapter NINE
comeback   84

chapter TEN
under pressure   96

chapter ELEVEN
captain sensible   107

chapter TWELVE
saviour   120

chapter ONE
off

The card was red. But even before that fateful 47th minute, the contest between England and Argentina would have been remembered long afterwards.

From the first whistle, the match had gripped the imagination and quickened the pulse. It had witnessed the goal of the tournament and disputed penalties for either side.

In its opening 45 minutes alone, it provided more incident than any of the 54 previous ties in the 1998 World Cup in France. Here was irrefutable evidence of why football at its best is the most compelling spectator sport on the planet. The searing pace at which England and Argentina conducted the game enhanced rather than diminished the skill and technique on display.

The Geoffroy Guichard Stadium in St Etienne

provided a stage that evening for arguably the two most irresistible strikers in the competition. For the South Americans, there was Gabriel Batistuta, a forceful and imposing forward, instantly identified by his flowing hair.

Michael Owen, for England, could hardly have provided more of a contrast. But the 18-year-old's slight stature was deceptive; he possessed the turn of pace of an Olympic sprinter and a cold-eyed detachment in front of goal.

The World Cup second round clash offered a global platform for another richly talented England youngster. Like Owen, David Beckham had been made to wait for his chance in the tournament by team coach Glenn Hoddle. Like Owen, he had forced his way into the starting line-up for this match with a spectacular goal in a previous tie. Like Owen, this would be the most momentous night of his life so far – but for reasons that could not be further removed.

England had endured a nightmare start to the match. After only six minutes Argentina were awarded a penalty when David Seaman rushed from his goal line and made enough contact with the legs of the oncoming Diego Simeone for him to fall. Batistuta stepped up to convert the spot kick.

But within four minutes England drew level, after

Owen went down under a challenge by Roberto Ayala in the opposing penalty box.

Alan Shearer provided as reassuring a sight taking the spot kick to English fans as Batistuta had to their Argentinian counterparts, and he was just as emphatic in his finishing.

But this opening exchange of goals was merely the overture. After 16 minutes, England went ahead with a goal never to be forgotten.

It was Beckham who started it all, teeing up a pass for Owen. The Liverpool forward accelerated towards the frantically retreating Argentinian defenders, all of them reluctant to either commit themselves or to try and match his blistering speed. First Jose Chamot and then Ayala were left in his wake.

For a moment, it looked as if Owen might lay the ball off to Paul Scholes. But if the notion ever entered his head, he discarded it in an instant. Then, just as quickly, he fired the ball across the advancing goalkeeper, and beyond him: 2-1.

Injury time was a minute old in the first half when Argentina equalised from a clever and obviously rehearsed free kick. Batistuta ran over the ball, and Juan Sebastian Veron rolled the ball to Javier Zanetti, who had stepped away from the distracted England defensive wall to drill the ball past Seaman.

At half time, 26 million television viewers back in Britain drew breath.

Diego Simeone had been an irritant to England's midfield, including Beckham, throughout that first half. He was a past master at the fractionally late tackle; the tug on the opponent's shirt that the referee didn't notice.

Two minutes into the new half, Simeone clattered into Beckham, bringing him down. There was nothing surreptitious about this challenge; the Danish referee Kim Milton Nielsen was standing only yards away.

As the match official walked towards Simeone to book him, the prostrate Beckham, still face down on the pitch, lifted a foot and clipped the Argentinian's leg. Simeone crashed theatrically to the ground as if he had just been shot.

It was evident from the numerous replays afterwards that Beckham's backward flick carried no force. His Manchester United manager, Sir Alex Ferguson, later said that it 'wouldn't have broken an egg.'

Sir Alex was right. But while Beckham's action might have carried no physical weight, the intent behind it was transparent. And FIFA, the World Cup's organising body, had stipulated from the outset of the competition that any retaliation should carry an automatic punishment.

Beckham regained his feet in time to see the referee pulling out a yellow card. He thought he was about to be booked. But that card was shown in Simeone's direction.

It was swiftly followed by the red, brandished above Beckham's head. Disbelief and distress fought for control of his expression as he turned and trudged towards the touchline.

While his team-mates prepared to resume their now unequal contest against Argentina, Beckham headed for an empty dressing room. He would find himself in far lonelier places in the months to come.

chapter TWO
chase lane dreamer

There was never any doubt that he was going to be a footballer, certainly not in his own mind. And those who got to know him rapidly came to the same conclusion – especially after they'd seen what he could do with a ball.

Put him behind a desk in a classroom and David Beckham retreated into anonymity. Put him on a football pitch, and you noticed him instantly. It was the one place where he could feel entirely confident of his abilities, and where, temporarily at least, he could forget any other concerns. Years later, at the lowest point of his career, the simple act of playing would provide him with exactly the same sort of escape.

From the moment that David Robert Joseph Beckham was born in Leytonstone, East London on May 2 1975, his destiny lay in football. Ted Beckham made sure of that.

By trade, Ted was a self-employed gas engineer. But while that paid the wages, football was his passion. He had been a useful non-league player for Barking, and had a trial with Leyton Orient. The hopes and aspirations he'd once entertained of a professional career in the sport were immediately transferred to his son.

Ted passed on to David one other lifelong obsession: Manchester United. Despite being a Londoner by birth, Ted had followed United since his schooldays in the Fifties and Sixties.

Now United have supporters all over the country, and fans of opposing teams often accuse them of merely jumping on the bandwagon of a successful club. But at that time, Ted's refusal to show allegiance to one of the London clubs he might have been expected to support was regarded as convention-defying. Another case of like father, like son, perhaps?

David's mum Sandra, a hairdresser, also came from a family deeply imbued by an obsession with football. Her father Joseph West is a Tottenham Hotspur fan and season ticket holder.

This could create tensions, not least at Christmas. Along with a new football, David's mum and dad bought him the latest United kit every year, while his grandad's present would invariably be the new Spurs strip. But while David has always been very close to his grandad, there was never any real doubt about where his true loyalties lay.

Nor was there any doubt about where David could be found from a very early age. He became a fixture at his local park, Chase Lane, heading there the moment he returned home from school.

It was there that his dad's advice on perfecting his technique was applied. While he played with friends for the sheer fun of it, there was always a more serious motive on his part; long after the friends had gone, David was still there, practising. Here was the forging of another permanent character trait.

One of his favourite pastimes was playing 'keepy-uppy' as he called it – juggling the ball with his feet, and head, chest and knees, often for hours.

An old family friend, Don Wiltshire, who used to train David, recalled later: 'When I first met David I asked him to juggle the ball with both feet. He only managed it a handful of times. I told him to come back when he could do it properly.

'A few months later he came back and did it about 2,000 times. He was that dedicated, even as a kid.'

David played football at every opportunity, and when he didn't, he was watching it. He went to see his dad play for local teams, and then persuaded him to practise with him afterwards.

'Dad was always there when I wanted someone to kick a ball around with,' said David. 'My mum would be dead worried because it would be 11 o'clock at night and we still weren't home from one of Dad's Sunday league matches.

'But it was only because I hadn't practised my free kicks and corners enough. I used to beg him to stay on and be in goal for a few more.

'Dad instilled so many things into me – keep improving, keep practising, keep your love of the game. And, as one of their greatest fans, to make sure I signed for Manchester United.'

Remembering his dad's playing days, David would joke later: 'He was known as "The Offside King." In fact, he got a trophy one year from some club for being offside more than anyone else in the league!'

Beckham Senior was also noted for occasionally letting his temper get the better of him on the field of play. 'I used to go and watch him the whole time and, though he used to try and tone it down for me, it never worked,' said David. 'So that's where I get it from.'

If David visited his grandparents with his mum, he would play football in the park next to the block of flats where they lived. And over the years he would play for his school, the Cubs, the Scouts, and his county.

The first team that David turned out for, at the age of seven, was Ridgeway Rovers. They were based near his home in Chingford, Essex, and played in the Enfield District League. David was selected along with 13 others to form the side from an open trial of 42 youngsters.

The Sunday morning matches became the highlight of David's week, along with the Wednesday night training sessions. One of his most enduring childhood memories was being grounded by his mum one Wednesday evening for something he had done wrong. It was the worst punishment she could have handed out.

'David was a talent from the moment he started playing,' remembered the team's manager, Stuart Underwood. So too were many of his team-mates. For three years Ridgeway Rovers didn't lose a single game.

Among them was Micah Hyde, who now plays for Watford. He twice beat David to Ridgeway's Player of the Year award. 'It was incredible to be part of a side that went three years unbeaten,' he said years later. 'Win, win, win was all we ever thought.

'For youngsters I think we had a great understanding between each other. We were completely attack minded and we always wanted to score.'

Even then, David stuck out for one particular reason. 'He was exceptional at dead-ball situations and you should have seen his corners! He would try the spectacular,' said Micah.

Jason Brissett was another team-mate who would go on to play professional football. 'David would take the free-kicks,' he also recalled. 'He was a natural. We would win by 10, 20, sometimes even 25 goals. We competed madly to be the top scorer.'

Over a period of three years, David scored an astonishing 101 goals in 115 appearances for Ridgeway. Manager Stuart Underwood also marvelled at the youngster's dead-ball skills.

'He could score from 30 yards time and time again. He would take the free-kicks and we knew it was a goal from the moment it left his boot. I remember one game when he was ten when he just coolly chipped the goalkeeper from 20 yards.'

Steve Kirby coached Ridgeway, and his son Ryan also played for the team. He would later remember a tour of Holland where, once more, David would exhibit his precocious talent. As the games there were not played on a full-size pitch, corners were taken from the edge of the penalty area. 'He could put them in the back of the net, no problem.'

The only reservation that Steve Kirby harboured

about David was his size – or lack of it. 'He had legs like a canary. He was a tiny lad,' said Steve.

Roger Smith agreed. He was a scout for Arsenal, and frequently watched the all-conquering Ridgeway team, and in particular its midfield star.

'He was technically very good,' said Smith later. 'But nobody could tell if he would fill out as physically as he has. He was a good striker of the ball, but very weedy.'

Jason Brissett noticed the same thing. 'My first memories of David are how small he was. The rest of the team towered over him. Everyone told him to eat loads of greens because he was so small.'

Another Ridgeway team-mate, Jason Lloyd, thought back to the original trial when he, David, and all the others had been selected for the side. 'He was so small I was surprised when they picked him. But from the moment I saw him play, I knew he was going to be good.'

So did everyone who watched David play. And that number was about to include one of the greatest legends ever to wear the Manchester United and England shirts.

chapter THREE
a ticket to the theatre

At last he was going to Old Trafford. He had seen it countless times on *Match of the Day*, and tried to imagine what it must be like.

His dad had arranged the trip. Ted had got tickets for David and a group of his friends to watch United at home in the League. Their opponents were his grandad's favourite team, and the club that most people in David's neighbourhood supported, Tottenham Hotspur.

Among those friends was one of David's Ridgeway team-mates, Nicky Lockwood. 'We were all on the terraces supporting Spurs except David, who was shouting for United. As soon as we got to the ground he was rushing off to buy their T-shirts, hats and flags. He was simply mad about them,' said Nicky.

Despite the 0-0 scoreline, the atmosphere at Old Trafford lived up to its nickname, 'The Theatre of Dreams', and to David's expectations. Scouts from the big London clubs like Arsenal and Tottenham might already be showing a distinct interest in him, but there was only one club for whom he wanted to eventually play.

It was while watching *Blue Peter* that the next opportunity to advance that dream presented itself. One of the items on the programme was about a soccer skills tournament organised by Bobby Charlton, one of the greatest players in United's history and England's record highest goalscorer. The final of the competition would be held at Old Trafford.

Hundreds of youngsters, who attended the Bobby Charlton Soccer Schools held all over the country, attempted to reach the final. David succeeded.

On December 7 1986, he found himself at last on the pitch at Old Trafford. The contest was held before United's latest League match, and Tottenham were again the opponents. The game would end in a 3-3 draw.

David and the other finalists faced a series of tests of their abilities including dribbling, ball-juggling and shooting. 'All the Spurs fans were there,' David would remember years later. 'As I was doing the dribbling in and out of the cones they announced that this was David Beckham from Essex.

'The Spurs supporters started singing and cheering.

But then the announcer said that I was a Manchester United fan. They booed me and I went into a couple of cones.'

Despite his modest recollection, the Spurs fans' reaction failed to knock David out of his stride. He won with the highest number of points ever scored in the competition. Afterwards, Charlton commented that David was the best 11-year-old he had seen in the six-year existence of his Soccer School. He told the crowd: 'Here we have a destined star.'

The prize was a trip to Barcelona to train for a fortnight with the then Spanish champions' youth team. At the time, Terry Venables was Barcelona's coach, and the club's two main strikers were Mark Hughes, a former Manchester United star who'd later rejoin the Reds, and Gary Lineker, who had become a national hero in England after finishing as the 1986 World Cup finals' top scorer in Mexico the previous summer.

David still keeps the photograph taken of him with Hughes, Lineker and Barcelona's midfield star, Nayim, who would later play for Spurs. 'Mr Venables gave me some advice then which I've never forgotten,' he said afterwards. 'He told me to practise, practise and keep on practising.'

Even then, David did not forget his loyalty to

Ridgeway Rovers. The team were involved in a local cup final, and David interrupted his holiday to fly back to take part. They lost.

By now, David trained twice a week with Spurs's youth team. He had been doing so ever since one of the club's scouts spotted him in January 1986 playing for Ridgeway.

'I used to go to Spurs and wear my United kit,' he said later. 'I was the only one who did and I got lots of stick about it. But I didn't care. I just wanted to be a United player. It's all I cared about.'

Indeed, his football skills had already merited an appearance in front of the television cameras. He was invited on to a daytime show called *This Afternoon* on ITV after winning the Bobby Charlton tournament.

Introduced simply as 'David from Essex' he proceeded to display to the studio audience the ball-juggling skills first learned long ago in Chase Lane park, and which had later so impressed Charlton.

Afterwards, the presenter, Sarah Kennedy, expressed surprise when David replied 'no' to her question about whether he had watched the big TV event of that year — the royal wedding of Prince Andrew and Sarah Ferguson. When she asked why not, his answer was typical. 'Because I was playing football in the park,' he said.

While continuing to pursue his ambition of a professional career in football, David earned extra money by working at the greyhound stadium in Walthamstow, East London. He was paid £2 per night to collect glasses and to empty ashtrays.

But his hopes took a knock when he was turned down for selection by England Schoolboys – because he was judged to be too small. Teacher Martin Heather, who coached David for Waltham Forest Boys and the Essex county team, said that David was denied a place after getting through trials to the final shortlist of 70 boys.

'I was told there was no way he was going to make it because he wasn't big enough for that type of game,' said Martin. 'Obviously skill and ability had little to do with it.'

While playing for Essex Boys however, David had already come up against other future stars. 'One game that sticks in my mind was the time I took Essex up to Liverpool to play Merseyside Boys,' said Martin Heather. 'We were 2-0 up and David was outstanding. But then along came this skinny little kid who scored two brilliant goals to help them win 3-2. It was Robbie Fowler.'

The England Schoolboys rebuff was a blow, but playing for Manchester United was what really mattered to David. Yet he feared that living so far away from the club could count against him.

Fortunately for him, Malcolm Fidgeon did not share that view. Malcolm was a talent scout for United, and happened to be at a match in Fairlop, Essex, in which David was playing. He immediately decided to recommend the teenager to United's manager, Alex Ferguson.

'He was very frail and tiny, but he could do things the other boys couldn't and I thought he wouldn't disgrace himself if he was given the opportunity of a United trial,' said Malcolm.

His mother Sandra would remember it years afterwards as one of the very few games that his dad could not attend. 'I stood there waiting because he was always the last out of the changing room,' she said.

'When he finally emerged, I just said: "It was a good job you had a good game." "Why was that?" he said. I replied: "The Manchester United scout was there and he's coming round to see us tonight."

'He jumped up in the air and cried because he always used to say: "I don't think they're going to find me down here."'

Now they had.

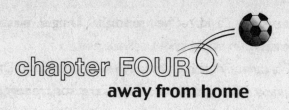

chapter FOUR
away from home

Even now the Beckham family still joke about it: who was the most excited when David signed schoolboy forms with Manchester United – him or his dad?

As a supporter of the club all his life, who had passed that burning allegiance on to his son and watched him develop as a footballer on countless Sunday mornings from the touchline, Ted was understandably delighted, but cautious. After all, most schoolboy footballers still fail to make the grade professionally.

David entertained no such doubts, at least not publicly. 'I gave up a lot when I was younger, going out with the lads, parties and discos, leaving my family. It wasn't easy, but I knew it was what I wanted to do. I never thought of anything else. I used to tell everyone and they'd laugh and say: "Yeah, but what else you gonna do?" I'd say: "No, football." United was the dream.'

Malcolm Fidgeon, the scout who had spotted David and recommended him to Alex Ferguson, recognised that determination in the youngster.

'Sometimes he got knocked off the ball because he wasn't big enough. But I was looking for a potential Manchester United footballer at 18 or 19, not at 14.

'For his size, David hit the ball extremely firmly but, more importantly, very accurately.

'At 12 he could take corners on full-length pitches and hit the penalty spot and was very accurate from set pieces.'

At the time David was also still training regularly at Tottenham Hotspur. But, as if his lifelong support for United was not enough, the differing attitudes shown towards him by Alex Ferguson and Terry Venables (who by now had left Barcelona and joined Spurs as manager) settled the matter.

'I think I met Terry Venables once in the two years at Tottenham,' David recalled later. 'That doesn't exactly inspire you to join the club.

'Manchester United were the most friendly club I went to, and that is what swayed me the most.

'Alex Ferguson was brilliant with me. His attitude certainly helped me when I decided to join his club.

Some managers forget who you are within minutes of meeting you.

'He always knew who I was from that moment to the day I first trained with United. They were the best at everything. The facilities and atmosphere are second to none. Spurs offered me quite a lot of money to sign, but I was sold on United.'

Malcolm Fidgeon drove David up to the trial. 'As we travelled together from Essex to Manchester he never showed his emotions much, but I could see he was excited and that there was a touch of steel about him,' he said.

'He did well at Old Trafford and Alex Ferguson was very helpful. He makes every boy feel part of things in an informal way, calling out things like: "Hey, Beckham, come over here. When are you going to grow a bit?"

'Alex knows the name of every trialist, even if he's only seen a list or watched a lad once. Believe me, he's outstanding when he's dealing with the kids at those type of sessions.'

Malcolm accompanied David again on the journey to Manchester the night before he signed for the club, and an unexpected hitch meant that they failed to keep an appointment with Alex Ferguson on time.

'We kept him waiting in a restaurant the day my wife Joan and I, David's parents Ted and Sandra, and

David himself took six hours to drive to Manchester for him to sign schoolboy forms at 14.

'We got stuck in horrific Friday night traffic but, when we eventually arrived, Alex was OK. He only wanted boys who truly wanted to play for Manchester United. I once asked David how badly he wanted to play for United and he replied: "Very badly."'

For the next two years, David spent every available spare moment, principally during the school holidays, travelling to Manchester to train at the club, and staying at halls of residence in Salford. It was the closest he had ever been to the heroes of his youth, in particular Bryan Robson, whose No.7 shirt he harboured the ambition of wearing one day.

Former United captain Steve Bruce would later recall a small, spiky-haired teenager who always seemed to be hanging around. 'Every time we went to London he was there, sniffing about,' said Bruce. 'One day in the dressing room at the League Cup Final he was picking up the boots and putting them in the skip just to be involved.

'We knew at the time that this kid must be a bit special just from the treatment he was getting.'

David didn't have to think twice when the manager offered him a deal as a youth trainee when he reached his 16th birthday. He signed on July 8 1991.

David was joining at an exciting time in the club's history. United had just won the European Cup Winners Cup, defeating Barcelona 2-1 in the final. Mark Hughes scored both goals against the Spanish club, which he had left in order to rejoin United. After years of under-achievement since the Sixties, when they won the European Cup under the management of Sir Matt Busby, Manchester United were at last winning trophies again under Ferguson.

David was also moving out from home for the first time, leaving behind his parents, his elder sister Lynne and his younger sister, Joanne, to travel up from Essex to live in lodgings. Settling in was not easy; he was asked to leave by his first landlady after a friend was caught taking food from the kitchen without permission, and just as rapidly left his second lodgings after complaining about the food. Finally, he moved in with a couple called Annie and Tommy Kay and would stay with them for nearly three years. The only time that he saw his parents was at weekends.

His London accent marked him out as someone different immediately. 'A lot of the local lads didn't like me when I first came,' said David years later.

Gary Neville, one of the fellow trainees who would become his best friend, recognised a misunderstanding about David that would pursue him throughout his career. 'People say about David that he's flash, he's got a nice car and nice clothes.

'But he was always like that even when he was on £29.50 a week. What you see now is what he was like at 14.'

Like all the trainees, David's only other money was £10 a week in expenses. They were also expected to undertake chores around the club, like cleaning the senior players' boots, sweeping floors, or serving behind the counter in the club shop one day a week.

At United's youth training headquarters in Littleton Road, Salford, David found himself surrounded by young players who were just as talented as him, and equally desperate to prove themselves worthy to be signed as a professional.

Former United defender Gary Pallister, who was at the club when David was a trainee, said: 'At United the kids are hungry for success – that's just how it is. You're not just playing against other teams but against other people coming through at the club. You have to earn your place, otherwise you're out of the team. And once you've been at Old Trafford, there's only one place you're going and that's down.'

David understood that the risk involved at United – it was harder to make it there than anywhere else – was part of the attraction. 'I came north from London leaving a lot of mates behind,' he said. 'It could have been hard if things didn't work out.'

'My entire career was on the line and the obvious dilemma at United was about first-team opportunities. I was confident in my own ability to get on, but never cocky about it.

'It can be quite intimidating coming to a club with players of international pedigree. It's even more difficult when you are a fan and you feel like getting the autograph book out.'

One of David's first priorities after joining United was developing his strength and size. He was still regarded as small and lightweight.

'David would stay behind after training and use weights to build himself up,' said Malcolm Fidgeon, who continued to check on his discovery's progress. 'On top of that, he enjoyed very clean living. He would be in bed by 9pm and was not distracted by the pull of pubs and clubs.'

That sort of discipline was drummed into the trainees from the moment they arrived at United. They were expected to be aware of the privileged position that they were in, and to be willing to sacrifice the late nights out enjoyed by their contemporaries elsewhere.

They were also taught not to argue with referees, not to complain or foul, to watch their diet carefully and eat properly, and to wear the club blazer.

Ryan Giggs represented the example that they all wished to follow. A star of the youth team already, the 17-year-old had recently broken into the first team and was already being hailed as the new George Best.

Alongside David in the youth team were other youngsters destined to be stars. They were mostly local boys, like Gary Neville and his brother Phil, Nicky Butt and Paul Scholes. Then there was Keith Gillespie (later to play for Newcastle United and Blackburn Rovers) from Northern Ireland. Other notable names included Robbie Savage, now playing for Leicester City, and John O'Kane, who would later join Everton.

They all came under the tutelage of United's formidable youth team coach, Eric Harrison. 'He was the guy who told me how important it was to come back in the afternoon and work on my own if I felt there were things in my game that needed attention,' said David.

He needed no second bidding. Just as he had as a boy in Chase Lane park, David was always willing to put in the extra hours of practice.

'That was the work ethic we have had pumped into us since we were apprentices. Me, Gary, Phil, Scholesy, Butty, Giggsy, we were brought up to work hard at our game and we knew the rewards in front of us if we did.

We had to go back in the afternoons and some of us went back in the evenings to work with the kids who were coming up when we were apprentices.'

Anyone trying to be too flash, however, soon incurred Eric Harrison's wrath, as David soon discovered during one youth team game against Liverpool. He was showing off instead of sticking to simple and effective balls to his team-mates. In the dressing room, he was fiercely reprimanded by Harrison, who accused him of playing 'Hollywood passes.' The lesson was learnt.

In 1992, the First Division Championship – the title which United had not won since the days of Matt Busby, George Best, Bobby Charlton and Denis Law in the late Sixties – eluded them again, when they were pipped by Leeds United. It was the also the final season for the Football League in its existing format; the following season the top clubs would break away to form the FA Premiership.

But there was one consolation for United. The youth team won the FA Youth Cup in 1992, the first time the club had won that trophy since 1964.

They defeated Crystal Palace over two legs, winning 3-1 in London, and then 3-2 at Old Trafford. David partnered Nicky Butt in midfield, Gary Neville was one of the central defenders, and Ryan Giggs was up front. Robbie Savage and Keith Gillespie were the substitutes, but the standard of the team was so high that at the time Paul Scholes couldn't break into the team.

The fantastically promising youth team was Alex Ferguson's insurance policy. David Pleat, then the manager of Luton Town, said at the time: 'Alex told me that the crop of kids he's got are the best the club's had since the Busby Babes. He's sitting on a gold mine.'

Some members of that youth team were now ready to break through into the senior ranks. But for David it would take longer than others.

chapter FIVE
physical education

David Beckham made his first team debut for Manchester United at a ground that no longer exists. The Goldstone Ground in Brighton, where a retail park now stands, was the modest setting for his big moment.

It was the night of September 23 1992, and United were defending the League Cup (or the Rumbelow's Cup as it was known at the time, after its then sponsors) in the second round of the competition at Brighton and Hove Albion.

The two teams' previous best-known meeting had been the epic 1983 FA Cup Final, which United won 4-0 in a replay after a 3-3 draw in the first game.

Nine years on, Brighton had fallen on hard times. They were in the Second Division, and in debt. Drawing United in a cup competition, with the attendance that it guaranteed, was precisely the sort of financial boost they required.

David was 17 years old and had been playing regularly in the reserves. But even after he was told that he was travelling down to Brighton, he didn't expect to get a game.

Afterwards, he would remember a scary flight in a small plane down to the south coast, and staying in the resort's Grand Hotel, which had been rebuilt after the IRA bombed it in 1984.

United's teamsheet that night included Steve Bruce, Gary Pallister, Paul Ince and Mark Hughes. But although they were 1-0 up when David was finally brought on, they had struggled to assert their superiority over their humbler opponents.

He was sent on in the 71st minute to replace Andrei Kanchelskis. Two minutes later, Brighton equalised. The game ended in a 1-1 draw. David made sure he kept the shirt he had worn, as a memento. He still has it.

Any hopes he might then have entertained about winning more frequent senior opportunities were premature. David returned to appearing for the reserves and having to be content with being on the fringes of first team selection.

Then he was thrown in at the deep end – a UEFA Champions League tie against Galatasaray of Turkey in

December 1994. United's hopes of progressing to the knock-out stages of the tournament were minimal; a crushing 0-4 defeat in Barcelona followed by a 1-3 reverse away at Gothenburg of Sweden had seen to that.

Even a United win against Galatasaray would be meaningless if Barcelona could get a draw at home to group leaders Gothenburg. Sensing their chances of success were remote, Alex Ferguson decided to gamble on youth. David and reserve team colleagues Gary Neville and Simon Davies were named in the first team.

For David it was not just the heady excitement of actually taking part in one of the great European nights at Old Trafford – his first big game at home. It was also an opportunity to play alongside Eric Cantona.

The Frenchman had arrived at United two months after David's first team debut at Brighton, and proved the crucial addition to the side, which finally won the club's first championship in 26 years in 1993. The following season United won the Premiership and FA Cup Double, prompted by Cantona's inspiration.

Like the rest of the United squad, David watched in awe at training sessions as Cantona showed off his bewitching array of skills. 'All the players look at each other and laugh because they know they couldn't do what he can with a ball,' said David at the time.

On the night United swept Galatasaray aside 4-0, and David scored his first senior goal. Simon Davies had already put United ahead, in only the second minute, scoring from a Gary Neville cross. In the 37th minute, Brian McClair had a shot blocked which rolled loose in the penalty area. Seizing his moment, David pounced and drove the rebound into the net.

In the second half, David played a significant role in United's next goal, nodding on a cross from Cantona into the path of Roy Keane who then scored. But, despite a late fourth goal, an own goal by a Galatasaray defender, it was not enough. Barcelona had got the 1-1 draw required at home to Gothenburg to take the group's second qualifying place. United were out of Europe again.

Even that could not dim David's memory of his goal, which remains as vivid now as it was on the night. 'We played in a practice match the day before the tie,' said David later. 'Eric was giving me advice, where to play, when to come in, what to do, and he was always there for me during the match itself.

'When I scored against Galatasaray, I couldn't describe the feeling. The first thing I remember is Eric coming towards me. We met in mid-air as I jumped to celebrate. I've got the picture hanging on my wall.

'Both my parents were at Old Trafford that night. My mum was in tears and my dad shot out of his seat and accidentally head-butted a bloke next to him.'

But still the first team opportunities remained few and far between. Fellow youth team graduates like Gary Neville and Paul Scholes were breaking through, but David was yet to make his League debut. One of the main reasons that he was being held back was because doubts remained about his physical strength.

Alex Ferguson decided to tackle the problem by agreeing to a request from lowly Preston North End in March 1995 to send David out on loan . David immediately feared that his days at Manchester United, the only club for whom he'd ever wanted to play, were numbered.

'To me, going out on loan was edging you out of the frame for United's future,' he recalled. 'In my eyes, that was what Alex was doing. But, in the end, it turned out to be a good experience.'

Best friend Gary Neville could tell what David was thinking. 'I knew he was worried at the time. He thought that was the end of him at Manchester United,' said Gary.

'It wasn't. The manager sent him there to toughen him up – and it worked. We all knew that David had great ability, but people said he was a bit soft going into tackles and headers.

'Being thrown into the Third Division with Preston – having people kick lumps out of him – toughened him up.'

Gary Peters, who was then Preston's manager, said: 'Alex believed the only ingredient missing from David's game was the physical aspect. There was no questioning his ability but they didn't believe he got stuck in enough.

'So when I asked Alex about taking one of his players on loan, he couldn't believe I wanted Beckham. I'd watched him in the youth team and been impressed. Then I saw him in the reserves and saw how good he was at that level.

'At the time he was behind lads like Paul Scholes, Nicky Butt, Keith Gillespie and the Neville brothers, but he had a bit more to his game than them.

'Fergie was surprised I wanted David and not someone like Gillespie. But he quickly agreed, saying he thought it would do the lad some good.

'I was a bit worried that David would struggle with the physical side. At this level you have to win the ball first and that means scrapping for it. At first I had to bully and cajole him a bit. But David soon got the message that he had to mix it with the hard nuts – and he learned quickly.'

David's debut for Preston was at their Deepdale ground against Doncaster Rovers. The game ended in a 2-2 draw, and it was David who scored the equaliser to earn Preston a point. The goal with which he did it instantly won over the Lancashire club's fans.

He scored direct from a corner. 'It was no fluke,' said Gary Peters. 'He hit it with such pace and accuracy the keeper didn't have a chance.'

In his next match, David struck again. 'He scored a free kick against Fulham that was pure class,' said Peters. 'It was a wicked bender and you knew you were watching someone very special.'

Peters had reached a verbal agreement with Ferguson to keep David at Preston for three months. But after only five appearances in one month, he was recalled by United.

'United watched every one of his five games for us so I wasn't surprised when Alex rang and said he was taking him back.'

Preston's fans were devastated at the prospect of losing the boy wonder who had suddenly landed in their midst. They wanted the club to ditch plans for the building of a new stand costing £4 million, and give the money to United to buy David instead.

David admitted afterwards that he was almost sorry to leave Preston. 'I met a lot of people there and made a lot of friends and I go back when I can,' he said later. He was also concerned that after his taste of first team League football, he was now about to return to life in the reserves.

His fears were misplaced. Alex Ferguson was short of midfield players. And so, a week after turning out for Preston North End at Lincoln City in the Third Division watched by a crowd of 5,487, David stepped out in front of more than 40,000 fans to make his League debut for United at home to Leeds United on April 2 1995.

The match ended in a 0-0 draw. A report in the *Guardian* newspaper summed up his appearance by commenting: 'Although the 19-year-old Beckham did well on his Premiership debut, he could not be expected to provide the service that Cole has come to expect from Kanchelskis.'

By the start of the 1995-96 campaign however, David had still played more first team football for Preston North End than he had Manchester United. The new season would change that. Over the previous summer the manager had dispensed with a number of experienced players, including Paul Ince, who had gone to Inter Milan, Mark Hughes, who'd gone to Chelsea, and Andrei Kanchelskis, signed by Everton. David made more than 30 senior appearances, as Ferguson began to regularly play the youngsters who had grown up together in United's FA Youth Cup-winning team

Doubts that Ferguson might be relying too much on their inexperienced young replacements seemed to be confirmed on the opening day of the new season, when United were defeated 1-3 at Aston Villa. This prompted BBC1's *Match of the Day* pundit Alan Hansen's now famous declaration: 'You don't win anything with kids.'

For the first two months the team was also without Cantona, who had been banned after aiming a flying kick at a spectator in a League match at Crystal Palace, narrowly avoiding a jail sentence.

But after a shaky start, which also saw them eliminated from the UEFA Cup early on by unknown Russian team Rotor Volgograd, United hit their stride. Inspired by Cantona's return, they clawed back a 12-point lead at the top held by Newcastle United, to win the Premiership.

In the FA Cup, they met Chelsea in the semi-final. David only played because of injuries elsewhere in the team, and he made the most of it.

His pass started the move that led to United's equaliser after they had gone a goal behind to Ruud Gullit, and in the 59th minute David intercepted an under-hit back pass and drove the ball beyond the reach of the Chelsea keeper. He had sent United through to their third successive FA Cup Final.

And, as it turned out, their second League and Cup Double in three seasons. United defeated Liverpool 1-0 at Wembley, with another Cantona wonder goal, scored from David's corner with less than five minutes remaining. He had nearly opened the scoring himself after only five minutes with a shot that was goal-bound until it was blocked by goalkeeper David James.

A minute from the end of the match, David was substituted with Gary Neville. His job was done. He had ended his first full season with Premiership and FA Cup winners' medals.

Watching high up in the stands was his dad, Ted. 'I cried at the Cup Final watching him come out,' he said afterwards. 'I've seen every final on the telly and it's something when you see your lad come out at Wembley.'

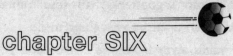

chapter SIX
even Pele never did that

'There's no argument David Beckham's unbelievable strike will be the goal of the season. The only debate is whether it is the greatest goal ever.'

So said the match report in the *News of the World* the day after *that* goal. Overnight it transformed him into the most talked about player in the English game.

It happened on Saturday August 17 1996, at Selhurst Park, where Wimbledon were playing Manchester United. The new season had just begun, and United were evidently picking up where they left off in the previous one.

Eric Cantona had opened the scoring, and Denis Irwin later made it 2-0. The match was already effectively won. But for David it was not over yet.

He picked up a loose ball while still inside United's half of the pitch and looked up. In the same instant as he spotted Wimbledon's goalkeeper Neil Sullivan off his line, David decided what he was going to do.

He was 57 yards away from the Wimbledon goal when he struck the ball. Inside the ground, the 25,786 fans suddenly realised that this was no speculative but hopeless punt upfield. It dawned on them that he knew exactly what he was doing. At the same time, it dawned on the increasingly panic-stricken Sullivan that the ball was sailing over him and into the roof of his net.

Asked about the goal afterwards, David said: 'It changed my life. It seemed to be in the air for hours and it all went quiet.

'Then the goal went in and it just erupted. I was on cloud nine. I wanted to shake everybody's hand and stay out on the pitch for half an hour.'

Comparisons were immediately drawn between David's wonder strike and the audacious attempt from a similar distance made by Brazilian legend Pele in a 1970 World Cup tie against Czechoslovakia. Pele, however, had missed.

Alex Ferguson was jubilant. 'You have seen the goal of the season already,' he declared. 'I have never seen it done before. Everyone in the dressing room has been scratching their heads trying to think of a goal like it. Pele is the only one who came close to doing the same.'

David receives the Manchester United Player of the Year Award, August 1997.

Manoeuvring the ball past Liverpool opposition during the FA Cup Final clash, May 1996.

A red card in the 1998 World Cup match against Argentina. David was later blamed by some for England's defeat.

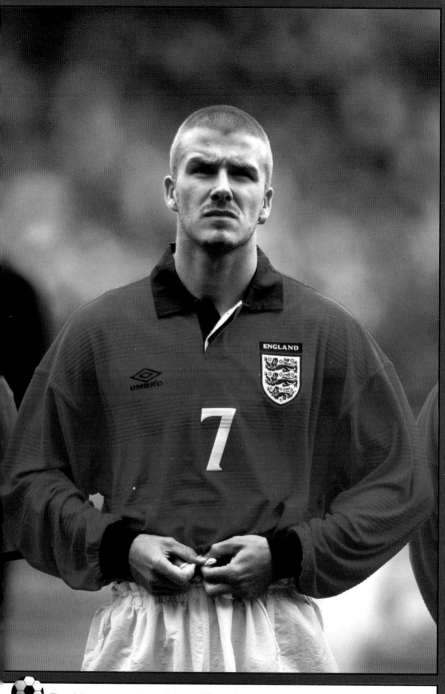

Beckham psyches himself up for the England v. Germany World Cup Qualifier, October 2000.

David and Victoria Beckham enjoying a night out at the 2nd NRJ Radio Music Awards.

David relaxing with wife, Victoria, at a party to celebrate their son Brooklyn's second birthday.

 Model superstar, David Beckham, showcasing designer sunglasses.

Captain of England in action during the England v. Albania World Cup Qualifier, September 2001.

Celebration as Beckham scores a stoppage-time equaliser during the England v. Greece World Cup Qualifier, October 2001.

David's dad Ted revealed after the game that what had meant the most to his son was the congratulations he received from Eric Cantona. The Frenchman had congratulated him with the words: 'Beautiful goal, David.'

'It's the best goal I've seen and I don't suppose there will ever be a better one,' said Ted, who watched the match with David's mum Sandra and younger sister Joanne.

'I remember him getting the ball and having a go. I thought: "Oh no, what's he doing?" I just didn't think it would come off against a Premiership team and, anyway, it looked to be heading over the bar.

'But it twisted and dipped into the net. I didn't see it because fans in front stood up. But when I heard the roar, I knew. Joanne turned to me and said: "I can't believe he's scored from there, Dad."'

The family rushed to congratulate David after the match. 'I gave him a hug and said: "brilliant goal, son"' recalled Ted. 'He replied: "Yeah, it wasn't bad, was it Dad? I didn't think it was going in. It took ages to hit the net."

'It was as though he had done nothing – but that's the sort of lad he is, very level headed.'

It was a sign of how far he had come that David had begun the season by almost upstaging not just

Cantona, but in the FA Charity Shield match at Wembley against Premiership runners-up Newcastle United, Alan Shearer, too.

Shearer was making his debut for Newcastle, following his £15 million transfer from Blackburn Rovers. But he and the rest of the Magpies were swept aside in a 4-0 rout. David set up the first goal for Cantona, crossed for Nicky Butt to score the second, and then took a pass from the Frenchman to hit the third himself.

Among the spectators at Wembley was England's new coach, Glenn Hoddle. He had replaced Terry Venables that summer, after the latter had been unable to agree a new contract with the Football Association.

The whole of England was still talking about Euro 96 – the European Championships that it had just hosted – in which the home country had been defeated by Germany on penalties yet again in the semi-final.

Like every other supporter of the national team, David had been entranced by England's progress in Euro 96, and not just because two of his best friends were in the squad. But he had been watching in slightly different circumstances from most fans, as he was captaining the England Under-21 squad at a tournament in Toulon, France, at the time.

'I would be lying if I didn't look at Gary and Phil Neville during the summer and say I wasn't jealous of them being in the full squad,' said David. 'But I was privileged to captain the Under-21s and just have to accept it has taken me longer to make the step up than Gary or Phil.'

In the same match report in which it had enthused about David's goal against Wimbledon, the *News of the World* insisted: 'If he doesn't win an England call-up from Glenn Hoddle soon, there's something wrong.'

The newspaper needn't have worried. Hoddle had already had his card marked about David's abilities by Graham Rix, whom the new England boss had appointed to take charge of the Under-21s in Toulon.

Rix, a coach at Chelsea where Hoddle had previously been manager, said: 'You can look at players of that age and tell the ones who will fail, who will make it and those who will be stars. Becks is going to be a true star.

'Everybody knows what he can do with a ball at his feet, but that's not as important as what goes on away from game situations. Tell him something in training and it's done instantly, ask him to do something and there's no moans, raised eyebrows or questions. He just gets on with it.'

Rix added: 'He's still learning his trade, but give him

five years and I think Alex Ferguson will regard Becks as his general.'

Hoddle acted upon Rix's praise and named David in his first squad as England manager, for the opening tie in the qualifying group for the 1998 World Cup, against Moldova.

For the 21-year-old it meant that he would not only be rubbing shoulders with such stars of Euro 96 as Alan Shearer, Paul Gascoigne, David Seaman and Paul Ince. He would also be meeting the man who, along with Bryan Robson, was his biggest childhood idol: Hoddle.

The new national manager had been the most gifted English midfield player of his generation, but the England managers of his time had always seemed to find it difficult to accommodate his supreme individual skills within their teams. Consequently he had never played the number of internationals that his talent merited.

Hoddle's selection of David appeared to be a statement of intent that he was not about to make the same mistake. At a press conference shortly after the squad was named, David was asked which players he'd idolised as a youngster. Motioning in the direction of the man sitting next to him, he replied: 'I've always admired the boss and the way he played.'

'Good answer,' said Hoddle.

David's international debut in Kishinev, the capital of the remote eastern European republic, was marked by a 3-0 victory, and while he did not get on the scoresheet, his promising performance had done enough to establish himself in the England team.

His emergence as the country's leading young player brought its own swift rewards. United agreed a new and not surprisingly much improved five-year contract with David. Sportwear manufacturer Adidas signed him up to a boot sponsorship deal. And haircare company Brylcreem agreed a stunning £1 million advertising deal with him to update their product's image.

His capacity for scoring incredible goals continued, not least against Tottenham Hotspur in an FA Cup third round tie in January 1997, when his swerving free kick from just outside the penalty area curled over the wall of Spurs defenders and beyond their England goalkeeper Ian Walker. David's fellow professionals voted him Young Player of the Year. No wonder that his Old Trafford team-mates now nicknamed him 'Superstar.' Southampton and England star Matthew Le Tissier, claimed: 'He will dominate football for the next 10 years.'

And, to top it all, he was about to get a girlfriend

who enjoyed similar celebrity status.

Victoria Adams, otherwise known as 'Posh Spice' of the biggest selling girl band ever, The Spice Girls, met David in the players' lounge at Old Trafford after United had beaten Sheffield Wednesday 2-0 in March 1997.

They had first been introduced at a football match in London by her manager, and David kicked himself afterwards for turning away after only saying hello.

This time, at Manchester, Victoria was brought into the players' lounge as a guest, and went over to speak to David.

She later recalled what quickly attracted him to her. 'Unlike the other footballers who headed straight for the bar, David went straight over to his mum and dad. Someone who appreciates his family. I like that.'

On their first date, when she stood up to go to leave the room, so did David. He got up again when she returned. 'At first, I thought there was something wrong,' she said, 'and then I realised he was just being polite. I had never had anyone treat me like that. It was clear from day one he was a complete gentleman.'

Inevitably, it wasn't long before the press found out about them. But it was quickly evident that their relationship was much more than just a convenient publicity stunt for their respective careers. Like David,

Victoria came from a close-knit family background. Equally importantly, they obviously had a mutual understanding of the attention that fame brought.

'Having a girlfriend like Victoria does help me,' David admitted two months after their romance was publicised. 'We realised when we started going out that we would have to cope with certain things and because she is famous she understands those pressures. We talk about it a lot and help each other.'

But David insisted that their fame was not the reason they were together. 'I like Victoria for herself, not anything else,' he said. 'I'd like her if she worked in Tesco.'

He proposed to her on January 24 1998, and Victoria was so surprised that she asked him to do it again. 'I started thinking about proposing about a week after I met her,' he laughed later. 'But I'd had a funny feeling about Victoria before I even met her. I saw her on the telly and thought that if I could just meet her once, we'd be together for ever.'

Their relationship only served to magnify further the intense media interest that had grown around David. While Manchester United had failed in their latest attempt to win the European Cup, he had still become one of the most instantly recognised faces on the continent, not least because of the Adidas TV commercials, in which he was given the same billing as stars like Zinedine Zidane and Alessandro Del Piero.

England, meanwhile, had qualified for the 1998 World Cup in France, and David had been the only player to take part in every one of their qualifying matches. He appeared to be an established part of Glenn Hoddle's plans.

As the biggest football tournament on earth approached, David sought to maintain some perspective on his dizzying rise.

'In my career everything has come so fast it frightens me,' he admitted. 'I'm only 22. Sometimes people think I should be struggling more, but they don't understand that there's a lot of pressure at a club like this, plenty of younger kids coming through. You can't afford to have a bad game.

'I love the way of life in Manchester but the way of life for a footballer – the money and so on – can be frightening at times.'

Compared to what he was about to have to get used to, it was nothing.

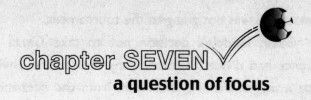

chapter SEVEN
a question of focus

The headline writers could hardly believe their luck. Only a week before the 1998 World Cup kicked off, David and Victoria were photographed leaving a restaurant in the south of France, where they had been staying with Sir Elton John. There was nothing unusual about that except for one particular: David was wearing a sarong.

The press had already taken a keen interest in David's fashion sense, especially since he had started seeing Victoria. But this was too good a chance to miss – '3 Lions On My Skirt' read the headline in at least one newspaper.

Only one other English footballer came close to attracting such overwhelming media scrutiny as David: Paul Gascoigne. He too had made the headlines in the weeks leading up to the World Cup, but for a different reason: he was not going to the tournament.

Glenn Hoddle's decision not to take Gazza to France had divided opinion. Many critics agreed with the manager, claiming that apart from the occasional flash of genius, such as the goal against Scotland in Euro 96, Gascoigne had never been the same player since the reckless challenge in the 1991 FA Cup Final that ruined his knee and nearly brought his career to a premature end.

But others believed that even if he was no longer the player he once was, Gascoigne retained that unpredictable quality that could turn a match. Many of the England players were among them.

After the World Cup was over, David said that he believed the decision to leave out Gascoigne was a mistake. 'I don't think there was a player in the squad who didn't think that Gazza should come, even if it was just to contribute 30 minutes in matches.'

What particularly concerned the England players was the manner in which Hoddle informed Gascoigne that he would not be going to the World Cup. Each of the players had to wait before being summoned to see the manager in his hotel room during a break in Spain to receive the good or bad news, without any inkling of what lay ahead.

'Leaving him out gave all the players a big shock but

I think it was the way the manager did it that caused the biggest problems,' said David. 'It affected the mood among the rest of the players. We were still talking about it in the weeks that followed, what a big decision it was, but also what damage it must have done to a mate.'

Gascoigne's performances during the World Cup of 1990 in Italy when England had reached the semi-finals remained vivid in David's memory. He had watched the tournament as a 15-year-old.

'Gazza was my hero,' David recalled. 'I dreamt then that I would reach that level, that next time I'd be there.'

Speaking on the eve of the World Cup, he could not know how prophetic his next words would be: 'What I'd love is to make the same sort of impact on this World Cup that Gazza made then. Everybody was talking about him after that.'

Despite the controversial build-up, England's World Cup squad provided a united front as they arrived in France to begin preparing for their group matches against Tunisia, Romania and Colombia. But if the treatment of Gascoigne had already caused David to begin revising his opinion of his childhood hero Hoddle, there was worse to come.

Rumours had been circulating in the week leading

up to England's opening match against Tunisia that David would be left out in favour of Tottenham Hotspur's Darren Anderton.

At first sight, this seemed an implausible choice. Over the previous season, David had made 50 appearances and scored 11 goals for United. Anderton, however, had managed only 15 matches for Spurs, and not scored once.

More pertinently, David was the only England player to feature in all eight of England's World Cup qualifying ties. Anderton had starred in none of them. In fact, he had turned out in only two internationals since Euro 96.

But Anderton seemed to have timed his return from the latest in a series of injuries just right. He was also a player whom Hoddle held in high regard, and he had conducted himself with distinction during Euro 96.

There had also been some talk that David's form had taken a dip over the previous Premiership season, during which he had finally inherited the No.7 shirt he had always longed to wear, following the surprise early retirement of Eric Cantona. United had finished the campaign with nothing – Arsenal winning the Premiership and FA Cup Double, and Monaco knocking them out in the European Cup quarter-final.

Then there had been the recent international

friendlies against Portugal and Saudi Arabia. On both occasions Hoddle had substituted David well before the end.

Hours before the team to face Tunisia was announced, David told one journalist: 'If I am not in the starting line-up I will be totally gutted. It will, without doubt, be the most disappointing moment of my entire career.'

His worst fears, however, were realised. Anderton got the nod from Hoddle, who claimed that David was not 'focused' for the match – something the player would later fiercely dispute.

'Personally, I didn't agree with the comment about me not being focused,' he said. 'I've been brought up to believe that whether you're playing on Hackney Marshes or in the World Cup, you give it everything you've got.

'My dad, my Sunday league managers – especially Stuart Underwood almost 20 years ago – and now Alex Ferguson have always stressed that to me. I don't start focusing when the whistle goes, I start on the Wednesday before Saturday's match, or sooner.'

David sat on the sidelines as England defeated Tunisia 2-0, and while his replacement did not have a particularly distinguished game, it was clear that the manager was not going to change a winning team for the next match against Romania.

Back home, Alex Ferguson professed himself puzzled by Hoddle's decision and offered words of comfort to David. 'Why reject Beckham, who is hardly ever injured and has tremendous stamina, in favour of somebody who is still trying to find his top-level game after long spells on the injured list?'

Three years previously, Ferguson had tried to sign Anderton, seeing him as the ideal replacement for Andrei Kanchelskis. Ironically, had Anderton made the move, David's career might never have taken off as quickly as it did, for it was Kanchelskis's unexpected departure which provided him with his opportunity to break into United's first team.

But now Ferguson was adamant about who he would pick for England were he in Hoddle's place. He admitted that Anderton 'is comfortable on the ball and probably has more ability to beat a man than Beckham.

'But Beckham is just about the best crosser of a ball in British football and he would be more likely than Anderton to score a goal for you.'

Ferguson reserved his greatest criticism of Hoddle for the way that David had been treated after it was announced he was not playing against Tunisia.

'Why was Beckham put forward for a mass interview with the media while he was still reeling from the shock of being left out of the team for the match with Tunisia? Those in charge of the squad's press arrangements should never have considered that and David himself should not have agreed to do it.

'He must have been devastated emotionally and asking him to bare his soul in public was not likely to help anybody but the headline writers. It is something I would never have allowed.'

However opportunity unexpectedly presented itself for David through an old friend's misfortune. Former United star Paul Ince was injured and came off after 33 minutes of the next match in Group G against Romania. David was sent on to replace him.

He was instantly aware of the tumultuous reception that he received from the England supporters in the ground at Toulouse, especially because it was such a contrast to recent internationals, like the game against Saudi Arabia at Wembley, when he and other Manchester United players had been jeered. 'I was totally overwhelmed. The reaction I got was absolutely staggering. Thanks to them I was immediately up for it and in the right frame of mind.'

David swiftly formed an effective partnership in midfield with the man who had been preferred to him: Anderton. But even they could not prevent Romania going ahead two minutes into the second half.

As the match ticked away, Hoddle sent on Michael Owen in the 73rd minute. Like David, the 18-year-old Liverpool striker had been overlooked by the manager so far. With seven minutes to go, Owen scampered into the Romanian penalty area and fired home the equaliser even as he was falling off-balance, finishing a move begun by David.

Disaster struck in injury time, when Dan Petrescu, who played his club football at Chelsea, cut in from the left flank, held off the challenge of Graeme Le Saux and then poked the ball through the advancing David Seaman's legs.

The defeat by Romania meant that England had to manage at least a draw against Colombia to be sure of qualifying for the World Cup's second stage. It also meant that Hoddle could not resist the popular demand for David and Michael Owen to be selected from the start.

England never looked like losing. Darren Anderton opened the scoring after 21 minutes, after Owen forced the Colombian defence into error. His pass to Anderton was dispatched with a rising volley into the roof of the net.

Nine minutes later, Paul Ince was brought down 25 yards from goal. 'I fancied it as soon as the free kick was awarded,' said David after the match. 'I just had that feeling inside me – I should have a crack. A couple of players asked me if I was going to and I said: "Just watch this."'

As David placed the ball, Paul Scholes joined the Colombian defensive wall. At the moment David shot, Scholes leapt from the wall, opening a space. The ball took a very slight deflection on the way, and swung in an arc way beyond the reach of the goalkeeper.

'From the moment I hit it, I knew that, if it was on target, it was going in,' said David. He wheeled away and ran towards the England fans behind the goalmouth in which he'd just scored, sliding on his knees with his arms aloft.

The only surprise was that England did not win by a greater margin. After the 2-0 victory, Glenn Hoddle provoked some incredulity with his insistence that he had planned to bring David in to the England team all along.

'We had always earmarked this game for David Beckham and Michael Owen because we thought that the Colombian back four would be susceptible to Owen's pace and that Beckham could free him with his passing,' claimed Hoddle.

Praising David's performance he added: 'I just felt that, in the early stages of the tournament, he was not quite there mentally. He is now.' David, who had already lost much of his respect for his former idol, kept his feelings on that matter private at the time. But he would later dismiss Hoddle's accusations about him as 'rubbish.'

What mattered was that England were through to the next stage. Everyone wanted to know about the free-kick against Colombia and how he had done it. 'Even now I will go out after training and spend a couple of hours with any of the apprentices who are still there, trying to get those free kicks absolutely spot on,' he said.

'It's something Alex Ferguson has always encouraged. He is always saying that if I want to be one of the best then I must practise, practise, practise.

'I even come in on my days off. I'll go to the training ground, take a bag of balls out and have as many shots as it takes before I am satisfied. It could be 50, it could be 100. And yes, I'm totally on my own.

'I don't need a goalkeeper or a defensive wall. Anyway, you know where they're going to be and at what height to kick the ball. Boring? No, it's the way I've been doing it for years.

'As a kid, I used to watch the Brazilians taking free kicks from all angles and thought: "My God, if only I could do that one day in the World Cup."'

And then came *that* match. Romania's late equaliser in their 1-1 draw with Tunisia ensured that they, not England, topped Group G. As runners-up, England's reward was to face one of the tournament favourites – Argentina.

chapter EIGHT
'one stupid boy'

On the eve of the England-Argentina clash, David's boot manufacturer Adidas ran a special advertisement in newspapers, which harked back to England and Argentina's previous meeting in the World Cup of 1986, when Diego Maradona had scored his infamous 'hand of God' goal.

Over a picture of David it carried the slogan: 'After tonight England v Argentina will be remembered for what a player did with his feet.' It got that right.

In the moments after the sending off, Glenn Hoddle stared straight ahead as David left the pitch. The first member of the England staff to offer consolation was masseur Terry Byrne, who put an arm around the player's shoulders as he disappeared down the tunnel.

He was ushered to the drug-testing room, an automatic procedure after every World Cup tie. 'It was a small, airless boxlike room where I sat on my own, feeling more upset than I have ever been in my life,' he said later that week.

David watched the rest of the 90 minutes on a television in the room. At one point, he went for a shower. While he was in there, Terry Byrne suddenly rushed in, shouting: 'Sol has scored!' For a moment David's spirits lifted, until Byrne returned to say the goal had been disallowed.

Campbell's 81st minute header from an Anderton corner, that seemed to have given England the lead again, was ruled out after Alan Shearer was adjudged to have used his elbow in the initial challenge for the corner. The decision cut short premature celebrations out on the touchline by several England players.

It was not the only blow they suffered. Early in extra time, the referee failed to notice a handball in the penalty area by Argentinian defender Jose Chamot. However, to be fair, he also took no action when Tony Adams accidentally handled in his own box ten minutes from the end of normal time.

But for most of the match after David's sending off, England were forced into a valiant defensive action. While every one of the remaining 10 men were outstanding, Adams, in particular, produced perhaps the greatest performance of his England career.

Before the start of extra time, David phoned Victoria. She was being filmed for a Spice Girls documentary at the exact moment that David's call came through, and viewers would later see her asking more than once what had happened.

At the start of extra time, he moved back into the tunnel where he stood to watch the rest of the match, out of sight of the crowd.

Argentina laid siege to the England goalmouth for the ensuing half-hour but the 'golden goal' that would have finished the contest at once would not come.

Just like the World Cup semi-final of 1990 and the European Championship semi-final of 1996, both of which had been against Germany, England faced the ordeal of penalties again.

Argentina went first and Berti put them one up. Shearer stepped forward to equalise. And then there was a chink of light for England. Hernan Crespo, who within two years would briefly hold the title of the world's most expensive footballer when he moved to Italian club Lazio, missed from the spot.

The hope was short-lived. England's next penalty taker, Paul Ince, also missed. Juan Sebastian Veron then converted his spot-kick, Paul Merson levelled the score again, and Gallardo of Argentina and Owen of England made the penalty score 3-3.

Roberto Ayala, the defender who had been so wrong-footed by Owen for England's second goal in normal time, made amends by beating David Seaman with Argentina's fifth penalty. Up stepped David Batty for England.

Batty, the terrier-like midfielder who had made way for David in the previous match against Colombia, had come off the bench in extra time to replace Anderton. Whatever his many qualities, he was the first to admit that penalty-taking did not rank high among them.

His run-up was unconvincing and his kick was even more so. It was safely stopped by goalkeeper Carlos Roa. Argentina were through to the quarter-finals, to meet Holland. England were going home.

'That was worse than anything else,' said David. 'It was then that I fully realised just what I had done. I kept thinking to myself that if I had still been out there I would have been one of the penalty takers.

'I could hardly bear to watch as they were being taken, and I really felt for Paul Ince and David Batty who never normally take penalties.'

David was the first of the team to return to the dressing room. 'The atmosphere was quiet and subdued. I went around apologising to my team mates. The mood was really sombre until Tony Adams said loudly: "Well done everybody."

'Then he came over to me and said: "Don't you ever think that you have let us down. You are a great player and I love you to bits."'

Adams' kindness meant a great deal to David. 'I will always remember it,' he commented. Nothing else was said in the dressing room.

Outside it, however, everyone had plenty to say. Former England manager Bobby Robson said of David: 'He will regret it for a long, long time.' His parents, who had been at the match, appealed for people not to over-react. 'You can imagine how we're feeling,' said his mum Sandra. 'But David hasn't let us down. We're still very proud.'

His dad Ted added: 'David's a brilliant player, don't forget. I hope fans stand by him. I spoke to David afterwards. He was choked, and just couldn't speak.'

David admitted that seeing his parents outside the ground after the match was the moment when he was finally overcome by emotion. 'I had not cried like I did then since I was a child,' he said. 'For a good 10 minutes, I just lost it.'

Glenn Hoddle's immediate post-match comments came under particularly close scrutiny. 'With ten men we defended like lions,' he said. 'It's a bitter, bitter pill to take and we are absolutely distraught but proud at the same time.'

Asked about David's sending off, Hoddle admitted: 'That cost us dearly. I am not denying it cost us the game.'

In the midst of its castigation of David for his sending off, some sections of the media seized critically upon Hoddle's remarks. 'The England coach has already infringed one of the unwritten rules of the game by suggesting that Beckham's exit probably cost his side the game,' claimed a report in the *Guardian* newspaper.

'Alex Ferguson, Beckham's manager at Manchester United, would never have allowed himself to level such an accusation at one of his own players, however provoked.'

The day after the Argentina match, Hoddle was sounding more supportive. 'It is his reaction that is now important,' he said of David. 'He is 23 with a wonderful talent and a great future. It was a silly mistake and I think the lad will learn from it. He's got to learn from it' said the England manager.

'I would plead with people to think about the positive things he's done in an England shirt. There was a fantastic performance on the night by 10 men who stayed on and David put in a fantastic performance against Colombia.

'The evidence is there for everybody, David Beckham more than anybody, to see how much it hurt.

There is hurt for him as an individual and us as a team. Nobody has to sit down and explain that to him. He's obviously going to take that on board. He is strong. You don't have to be ranting and raving on the field to be a strong character. But we've got to keep this balanced.

'He will be a wonderful talent for England and Manchester United over the next few years. I think his club and anyone that can help, should. But it would be wrong for too many people in football to put blame on his shoulders.'

Even the Prime Minister Tony Blair urged the country not to blame David for England's departure from the World Cup. 'I should think that no one feels worse about it than David Beckham does, and he is obviously going to have to learn from that,' he said.

Alex Ferguson confirmed the truth of that. 'I made sure I talked to David Beckham on the morning after the worst night of his football career,' he said. 'He was as low as I expected him to be.

'All the horrible implications of his moment of stupidity against Argentina had really got to him by then and I could sense that he just couldn't wait to be somewhere far away from the World Cup.'

That somewhere was New York, where he joined Victoria, who was still on tour there with the Spice Girls. He left behind an unprecedented campaign of vilification against him in England.

It was summed up by the *Mirror*'s front page headline the day after the Argentina defeat – '10 Heroic Lions. One Stupid Boy.' The newspaper also printed a dartboard on another page, with David as its bullseye.

The *Daily Mail*'s front page read: 'Moment of Lunacy That Cost Cup Hopes.' In an editorial the *Daily Telegraph* fumed: 'Beckham's silly little, smart little kick at his Argentinian opponent was what's wrong with the national character.'

In the *Sun* newspaper, one journalist wrote of David: 'The abiding memory of his World Cup now will be a rush of blood and a pointless attempt to kick out at Argentina skipper Diego Simeone.

'If it had not had such serious consequences, you would have thought he was back in the playground. To do it right under the nose of the referee just makes it even more crazy, especially after weeks of warnings about how officials would treat such matters at this tournament.'

The writer of the article then apologised publicly to Glenn Hoddle. 'The millions who were screaming for Beckham's inclusion at the start of the tournament – myself included – have to concede that you had a point when you claimed Beckham was not focused.'

David himself apologised in print a couple of days

after the match. Speaking to the *Sun* newspaper he said: 'This is, without doubt, the worst moment of my career and I will always regret what I did.

'I have apologised to my England team-mates and manager Glenn Hoddle and I want every England supporter to know how deeply sorry I am.'

He added: 'I do not want to make excuses but I certainly didn't feel it was a red card offence. When I saw the referee pull out a yellow I thought I was going to be booked, then he showed it to Simeone.

'I was absolutely staggered when he produced the red and sent me off. I felt sick and numb. I couldn't believe what was happening to me.'

The apology cut little ice with the prevailing national mood. One five-year-old boy was quoted as saying: 'I think David Beckham should be sent to his room with no supper.' A Kent couple called Dennis and Brenda Beckham was plagued by telephone calls from angry fans. 'It was funny at first,' said Mr Beckham. 'But after the first few calls it got a bit annoying.' His wife had the last laugh however. She told callers that David was out playing football.

The Bible Society called on the nation to show forgiveness to David, with the full backing of the Archbishop of Canterbury. 'David Beckham is a human being like you and me,' said the society's director,

Baptist minister Dr David Spriggs.

'Every day, all of us make terrible mistakes, in our homes and families, at our places of work, and in our local communities. Sometimes our actions make David's mistake look very trivial.'

The reaction to David's sending off began to take a more sinister turn. An effigy of him, dressed in an England shirt with his name on the back and a sarong, was hung outside a South London pub. Hate mail was sent to his parents' home.

A fortnight after England's World Cup exit, David's father finally spoke out about the abuse being directed against his son. 'He's made one mistake and been absolutely slaughtered for it,' said Ted.

'All he wants to do is play football. He'll go back to training but after that, I don't know. It's too early to say whether he'll stay in England or go abroad.

'I'm no longer proud to be British after what they've done to my son – all through a game of football. I'm just glad David's been out of the country. He hasn't seen half of what's gone on and I won't let him.'

Alex Ferguson was similarly protective. 'The way he was treated by sections of the media afterwards makes you wonder if the attitudes to sport in our country have gone totally insane,' said the Manchester United boss.

'Everybody knows that I can get pretty worked up about football,' he added. 'But I like to think I can maintain a perspective about the game and the rest of life. I was sickened by much of the cruel nonsense produced about Beckham last week. He could hardly have been more vilified if he had committed murder or high treason.

'There was a vindictiveness in many of the comments about Beckham that made it obvious he was paying yet again for being more of a celebrity than any other footballer in Britain.'

Ferguson also offered a fascinating insight into why David had reacted to Simeone's foul in the way that he did.

While conceding that the referee might have felt constrained to apply the letter of the law in sending off his young protégé, Ferguson claimed: 'I believe, however, that there was an extra factor at work and it relates to Beckham's tendency to react heatedly and lose his discipline when he feels opponents are taking liberties with him on the field.

'Lads like him, who play football and don't go around kicking people, often respond to rough treatment by trying to prove they are tough enough to stand up for themselves. Almost always they do it in silly ways and all it does is annoy the referee'

'At Manchester United we have made it clear to Beckham that he has to deal with this problem. I have tried to ram it home to him that it's a physical game where players of talent will always be singled out for a hard time. I have told him the only way to get back at the opponents who do that is by showing them he is better with the ball than they are.'

Ferguson also revealed that David had allowed his temper to get the better of him on a previous occasion at which the England-Argentina referee, Kim Milton Nielsen, had been in charge.

'It was during the second leg of our European Cup quarter-final with Porto in March 1997,' Ferguson remembered. 'We beat the Portuguese team 4-0 at Old Trafford and in the process of getting a goalless draw in the away match Beckham was caught up in a little off-the-ball incident in the second half and should have been booked.

'If Nielsen had given him a yellow card, he would have missed the first leg of the semi-final with Borussia Dortmund. I was convinced the referee was aware of that when he let Beckham off with a lecture.

'When the trouble occurred in St Etienne, Nielsen may have thought: "I gave you a break once and you don't seem to have learned from it – so this time you're off." Officials remember their encounters with high profile players.'

Returning to United later that summer, David was greeted by the sight of police patrol cars positioned at junctions on the approach to the club's training headquarters. He was pictured leaving his house peering anxiously out from under a black bobble hat.

Concern was expressed about whether the reception he was bound to receive at away matches would make it impossible for him to remain in England. Barcelona was reported to have made a £17 million offer to take him to Spain. Real Madrid, Juventus and Lazio were all said to be monitoring his situation with interest.

David got a taste of what was to come when he was booed throughout the FA Charity Shield match in August 1998 by Arsenal supporters. Worse still, Arsenal won. But in United's opening Premiership fixture of the season, at home to Leicester City, David started as he meant to go on.

United were losing 1-2 and the 90 minutes was up. Leicester gave away a free kick 25 yards out. There was only one person who was ever going to take it. David swerved it around the goalkeeper and levelled the score.

His first away match, at West Ham United, was the biggest test. David endured boos and taunts from a mob as he arrived with his team-mates at the east London club's Upton Park ground, and throughout the match was a target for some vicious abuse.

The officer in charge of policing the West Ham match was full of praise for the manner in which David handled all that was thrown at him. 'There have been enough stories willing to knock David Beckham, and it's time he got some praise,' said Chief Superintendent John Boylin.

'The professionalism of his reaction at West Ham on Saturday took the sting out of a potentially nasty situation. Even when he was sent flying by a tackle he didn't make a fuss and his approach was just as we would have wished.

'In fact, because of his actions, I think the stick he received was relatively gentle – I have certainly heard much worse.'

And that established the pattern for the rest of the season. David got on with playing football and refused to rise to the bait. The taunts and abuse swiftly began to die down – not least because United were embarking on what would be the most successful season in their history.

By the end of 1998, David was able to tell one newspaper that he did not feel guilty about the sending off against Argentina.

'Let's face it, I had never been sent off before and I haven't since. I'm not a violent person but there are times when you do react. I just get involved, but all footballers do because it is that kind of game.'

Nor, despite the reports, had he ever thought of leaving United. 'When I came home from the World Cup I knew I just had to get on with my life and ignore all the extreme criticism,' he said.

'It had crossed my mind that going abroad might be one way of getting some peace, but I soon realised that I didn't want to be anywhere but Old Trafford.'

Diego Simeone also admitted what had been obvious all along but forgotten in the uproar following the sending off. 'In reality he didn't do anything,' said the Argentinian. Asked whether the blow from David caused him to fall to the ground, Simeone said: 'It was possibly not so strong.'

But the best news that David had received came within 48 hours of his sending off – when he joined Victoria in New York. For it was there that she told him she was pregnant.

'There is no way I could have survived the World Cup aftermath without Victoria,' he said. 'That's why I went straight to New York to be with her. She didn't say a word when I saw her, just gave me a big cuddle.

'She was about a month pregnant – no one knew

except us – and was as pleased to see me as I was to
see her. No way did I expect things to turn out as nasty
as they did but, once I was with her, I knew I'd get
through it.'

chapter NINE
comeback

It was Sandra Beckham who came up with the idea of David making his peace with Diego Simeone.

United were due to face Simeone's club, Inter Milan, in the quarter-final of the European Cup nine months after the incident at France 98. David's dad Ted explained: 'I keep all the shirts David collects and I originally said that I wanted either Roberto Baggio's or Youri Djorkaeff's. Then his mum said: "Why not Simeone's?"

'When we went round to David's apartment his mum mentioned it and he agreed it wasn't a bad idea.'

And that is how it happened. David and his World Cup tormentor shook hands at the beginning of the home leg at Old Trafford, and then at the end David went and found Simeone and offered him his shirt. By that time, he had gained a more than satisfactory revenge on Simeone by setting up both the goals for United's new £12.6 million striker, Dwight Yorke, in a 2-0 win.

Alex Ferguson was ecstatic afterwards about David's performance. 'I thought Beckham was outstanding tonight,' he said. 'I didn't say anything special to him about the circumstances of the game, but he distinguished himself out there. No one matched him and there were some terrific players on that pitch.'

The following day, however, was marked by a much bigger milestone: Victoria gave birth to a 7lb baby boy in London's Portland Hospital. Interviewed outside the hospital, David said: 'This has topped everything off after the football last night. The feeling is great, but you can't compare the two.'

The couple decided to call their son Brooklyn Joseph. His first name was inspired by the New York borough where they first discovered that Victoria was pregnant, and his middle name was in honour of David's grandfather. This confounded the *Daily Star* newspaper, who had confidently reported four months earlier that the baby would be called Tyler.

David marked the birth of his first child a month later by having his son's name tattooed on his back. He also had 'Brooklyn' embroidered on pairs of his football boots. 'Being a father is just how I expected, totally as I expected,' he said. 'I knew I would enjoy it.'

He told another interviewer: 'I know a lot of things have been said about us being too young and not married and bad role models for young people. But we love each other, we're best friends and we're ready to be parents. I think that's a good example to set.'

By the beginning of May 1999, United were on course for an unprecedented Treble of FA Premiership, FA Cup and European Cup. No wonder then that 11 months after the sending off against Argentina, David was able to claim: 'My football life is perfect. My private life is perfect.'

He added: 'If you go through an experience like that, you can either crack up or make people eat their words. I just feel sorry for those who said the things they did. But I don't hate anyone.

'It was upsetting for my mum and dad and my friends, and Victoria was upset because I was. But now they know I am happier than I have ever been.

'It's not nice to be booed and jeered and I don't want people saying horrible things about me. All I was interested in was doing well on the pitch.'

He had certainly done that throughout 1998-99. As he said: 'I have enjoyed this season better than any other.'

So had everyone connected with United. The signings of Dwight Yorke, Jaap Stam from PSV Eindhoven of Holland for £10.75 million, and Danish winger Jesper Blomqvist from Parma in Italy for £4.5 million, had made the squad the strongest yet under Ferguson's management, and the return from long-term injury of club captain Roy Keane was the equivalent of buying another new player.

In the Premiership, United had put behind them an early season 0-3 defeat at the hands of their old rivals and the title holders, Arsenal. By the start of 1999 they were scoring for fun: four against West Ham, six past Leicester, and then eight against Nottingham Forest – including four from Ole Gunnar Solskjaer who only came on as a substitute ten minutes from the end.

The FA Cup nearly came to a premature end for United in the fourth round against Liverpool. Michael Owen put the Merseysiders ahead after only three minutes. With 88 minutes of the tie gone, the score remained the same.

Then United won a free kick. David floated it across the face of the goal, and Andy Cole headed it down into the path of his strike partner, Yorke, who scored. In the final minute, Solskjaer appeared again to hit the last-gasp winner. He was starting to make a habit of it.

The FA Cup semi-final replay with Arsenal was one of the most compelling matches that even that competition has witnessed in its 130-year history. The first match had not even hinted at what was to come, finishing goalless.

After 17 minutes, David put United ahead with a curling drive that would have been the goal of the game in most contests. Arsenal equalised after 69 minutes with a shot from Dennis Bergkamp which deflected off Jaap Stam.

In the last minute, it looked as if Arsenal would silence all the increasingly excited chatter about United winning the Treble. They were awarded a penalty, that Bergkamp took. Somehow, Peter Schmeichel in United's goal got down to push it away.

The tie went into extra time, where it was settled by a truly stunning winner. Ryan Giggs weaved in and out of the Arsenal defence before lashing a rising drive past David Seaman. It was the sort of goal that will be repeated on television for many years to come.

But it was the European Cup nights at Old Trafford that really electrified United's season. The club had been given a formidable draw in the group stage, up against two of the continent's giants: Barcelona and Bayern Munich.

United fought out two thrilling 3-3 draws with

Barcelona at Old Trafford and in Spain, and were also held home and away by Bayern. Putting eleven goals in two matches past the fourth group member, Brondby of Denmark, sent United into the quarter-finals where they would then dispose of Inter Milan – a 1-1 draw in Italy following their 2-0 victory at home in the first leg.

The semi-final pitched United against another legendary Italian club, Juventus, but even when Ryan Giggs scraped an injury time equaliser in the first leg at Old Trafford, the final still looked a remote prospect.

What followed was one of United's finest nights in Europe. After only 11 minutes of the return leg in Turin, the match seemed over, when Juventus took a two-goal lead.

But in the 25th minute, David's cross found Roy Keane's head to reduce the arrears. Nine minutes later, Yorke's diving header from a Cole cross levelled the scoreline, and six minutes from the end, with United already going through on the away goals rule, Cole made absolutely sure with a third goal.

United now faced an epic test of three matches in 10 days to complete the Treble. The first part was completed when they won the Premiership with a 2-1 victory over Tottenham Hotspur at Old Trafford, after going a goal down. David got United's equaliser, with a shot that Spurs' goalkeeper Ian Walker couldn't hold, and Andy Cole came off the substitutes' bench and grabbed the winner less than two minutes later.

Six days later, United walked out at Wembley alongside Newcastle United in the FA Cup Final. That was the nearest Newcastle got to United for the rest of the afternoon. Teddy Sheringham and Paul Scholes provided the goals in a 2-0 win, but it was David who particularly caught the eye for the way he ran the game from central midfield.

He had moved into that position when Roy Keane went off injured after only eight minutes. With Keane out suspended for the European Cup Final against Bayern Munich at Barcelona's Nou Camp Stadium, David was given the same role.

He worked tirelessly throughout the match, despite the close attentions of his Bayern midfield opponent Jens Jeremies. But elsewhere United had problems. In the absence of Keane and Paul Scholes, who was also suspended, Alex Ferguson had put Ryan Giggs on the right flank where David normally operated, and brought in Blomqvist on the left.

The tactics didn't work. Bayern went ahead from a well-worked free kick routine after only six minutes, and proceeded to stifle all United's invention from then on. Playing on the right meant that left-footed Giggs had to come in rather than go outside defenders, rendering him less effective, and Blomqvist was marked out of the game by Markus Babbel.

The Times wrote admiringly of David the following day: 'Apart from taking the corners and free kicks, governing a congested midfield, overlapping Giggs on the right flank where possible and prompting most of United's attacks – all of it while outnumbered by some of the most dogged competitors even Germany has produced – Beckham must have wondered if he should disappear early to brew up the half-time tea.'

David eventually moved back out to the right wing when Ferguson reorganised the team and sent on Teddy Sheringham and then Ole Gunnar Solskjaer to look for goals. But it was still Bayern who came closest, hitting the post and bar.

The most extraordinary comeback in the history of the European Cup has been well documented. For David it began as the final minutes ticked away.

'It was amazing. We were losing 1-0 and I looked around and saw the cup was on its way down with Bayern Munich's colours on it,' he recalled after the final.

'Yet two minutes later it was ours and I had it in my hand.'

David was instrumental in what happened in those intervening two minutes. Making another sortie down the left wing, he was blocked by Bayern midfielder Stefan Effenberg and the ball went for a corner.

Peter Schmeichel raced from his own penalty area into Bayern's just before David's corner swung over. Unsettled by the opposing goalkeeper's unorthodox presence, the German defenders struggled to clear the ball only as far as Giggs. He guided the ball through to Sheringham inside the six-yard box who bundled the ball home.

From the restart, Solskjaer brought the ball back upfield deep into the Bayern half. It was cleared for another corner. David stepped up again. This time he found Sheringham, darting in between two defenders to nod the ball on to Solskjaer. His outstretched foot diverted the ball into the roof of the net.

There was barely time for Bayern to kick off again. After a 31-year wait United had their hands on the European Cup once more. David dedicated the triumph to Alex Ferguson. 'This is for him' he said. 'He deserves everything he gets. He brought me up and has made my career what it is. So we all owe the manager everything.'

Ferguson was mutual in his praise, saying of David: 'He has the best stamina in the club. The boy is just a great player. He has become a better player this season, but we expected that. He is 24 and approaching the mature years of his career.'

Other distinguished watchers were equally impressed. Kevin Keegan, who had taken over the England manager's job from Glenn Hoddle, claimed: 'If they ever start cloning footballers, David Beckham would be the first you sent to the laboratory.'

Pele, who was in Barcelona for the match, called David: 'one of the very great players of this year,' adding: 'He is a very important player for the team. He works very hard, he has good vision, good movement and good delivery.'

The most eventful and ultimately successful 12 months in David Beckham's life was capped by his marriage to Victoria in Ireland on July 4 1999. The couple exchanged vows in front of only 29 people, including their immediate families and closest friends, with Gary Neville as best man, at Luttrellstown Castle in Dublin.

Most of United's victorious Treble-winning squad travelled over for the reception for more than 200 guests afterwards. Millions more eagerly awaited the first pictures of the event in the magazine that had signed a £1 million deal with David and Victoria for exclusive rights to their wedding photographs.

The couple's celebrity lifestyle enthralled the press. Their new £2.5 million home in Hertfordshire was immediately dubbed 'Beckingham Palace.' Then there was David's dazzling collection of expensive cars. They were a far cry from his first set of wheels – a Ford Escort provided by the club, that had previously belonged to Ryan Giggs.

Among the cars he drove now was a £145,000 Bentley, a Mercedes convertible, an Aston Martin DB7 costing £92,000, and a Ferrari 550 Maranello that had been a gift from Victoria, and retailed at £200,000.

Nor had any footballer ever had his fashion sense picked over in such close detail. Since the sarong, he had been seen out in numerous designer labels, from Gaultier and Gucci to Vivienne Westwood. There had been woolly hats, a knitted Tibetan peasant hat, and then there was the famous bandana.

David was seen in the £75 silk headgear on a night out with Victoria at a launch party for a jewellery collection by Jade Jagger, daughter of Rolling Stones singer Mick. It took place on the eve of United's trip to Austria to face Sturm Graz in a group match in the 1999-2000 European Cup. As a result of his being there, David was reportedly fined by United £50,000.

It was only the latest incident to have made the start to the season after the Treble a less than auspicious one for David. He was seen making a two-fingered gesture to Leeds United fans at Old Trafford, and there were allegations of retaliatory action in incidents at matches in the Premiership and the European Cup.

The general impression was of someone struggling to cope with the enormous pressure of being the most talked about and watched player in the country. While taking no direct action, an FA official did hold a meeting with David at which the importance of him not giving in to provocation was impressed upon him.

David was also forced to deny reports that Victoria had claimed he wanted to leave United and play abroad. 'I've never talked about leaving. Neither me nor Victoria have talked about leaving Manchester United,' he told the club's own MUTV channel.

Then, just when he might have thought things could not become any worse, David got himself sent off again.

chapter TEN
under pressure

The trip to Brazil for the FIFA Club World Championship was ill-fated from the start.

The idea behind United's participation in the inaugural competition was that it would boost England's bid to host the 2006 World Cup. But the club came under sustained criticism from the English press for withdrawing from the FA Cup that they should have been defending to go to Brazil.

And once the squad arrived in South America, their troubles continued. The local media accused United of not taking the Club Championship seriously.

Any hopes that United might have entertained of putting their troubles behind them once they got on the pitch were soon dashed. Playing the Mexican champions Necaxa in their opening group match at the vast Maracana Stadium in Rio de Janeiro, they were a goal behind after 15 minutes due to a dubious penalty.

In temperatures nearing 100 degrees Fahrenheit, United struggled to get back in the match, and were booed throughout by the local supporters, whose team Vasco Da Gama were also in United's group.

Two minutes before half-time, David's badly mis-timed and high challenge felled Necaxa defender Jose Milian. He could have few complaints when the referee unhesitatingly sent him off.

United's evening went from bad to worse. A second penalty was awarded against them, although this time it was saved by goalkeeper Mark Bosnich. Even Sir Alex Ferguson (he had been knighted following United's achievement in winning the Treble) was sent off, when the referee ordered him from the United dug-out for his increasingly heated comments. Only a late penalty by Dwight Yorke, after a shot by Ole Gunnar Solskjaer was handled, spared United defeat.

In their next match against Vasco da Gama, United were without David who was suspended. They lost 1-3, and their final group match against Australian champions South Melbourne was meaningless, despite a 2-0 win. United were going home early.

David candidly admitted afterwards that he could be 'hot-headed.' 'It's hard for me to stay on the right side of the law because I have always been a winner and always wanted to win. You are so hyped up in games that you do lose control.'

One famous United old boy warned David of the dangers of having a short fuse. Sir Bobby Charlton, now a director at the club, said: 'He's actually done well since he was sent off in the England-Argentina game. He is under more pressure than anyone else, but he has to learn to handle it, it is as simple as that.

'There is always an opportunity for someone like him to explode if the situation is right. But he is a big enough lad to be able to look after himself.'

Former England manager Graham Taylor voiced a concern that David might follow in the footsteps of another United legend, George Best, by turning his back on the sport before his time.

As ever, David's dad Ted sprung immediately to his defence. 'I am just fed up with everything that has been written about David,' he exclaimed. 'He has brought a lot on himself but he is a young man.

'You can only take so much. I really don't know how he copes with it all, he is much stronger than me in that sense.

'Yes he has made mistakes but that is all part of growing up. Everybody keeps slagging him off about his cars and his clothes. What is wrong with it if he can afford it? If I had his money I would do exactly the same.'

Ted was also upset by newspaper claims that he and Sandra did not get on particularly well with Victoria's parents. 'One day, in the papers, it says we don't get on – and that night we are going round to the Adams for something to eat. We are always round there.'

But David's problems were not over yet. On the Friday before a Premiership clash at Leeds United, he failed to turn up for training. His explanation was simple. 'I felt I had good reason to miss training. Brooklyn was ill with gastro-enteritis. I rang the club and told them that.'

Sir Alex Ferguson, however, was not satisfied. He knew that Victoria had been seen out in London on the same day, suggesting to him that the little boy's illness could not have been that serious.

'I had to think that David wasn't being fair to his team-mates,' said Ferguson later in his autobiography. 'Nicky Butt, Phil Neville and Ole Gunnar Solskjaer cannot count on being regulars in our first team, but they are model pros who never miss training and I had to imagine how they would feel if David could adjust the schedule to suit himself.'

Ferguson had already resolved to leave David out of the team to face Leeds on the Sunday. But his attitude hardened still further the following day when

David did arrive at the club's training ground. There was a heated exchange between the two men, and David was ordered to leave.

'It disappoints me that a little argument between me and the manager was blown up out of all proportion,' said David after the event. 'In the end, I abided by what the manager and the club decided and accepted their disciplinary action.

'I've heard it said that I'm trying to be bigger than the club. I'm not and never could be. Nobody can be bigger than the biggest club in the world.'

Ferguson also quickly regarded the matter as closed. 'My decision to leave him in the stands at Elland Road became a bit of a drama, but it was quite straightforward to me. It doesn't matter to me how high a player's profile is. If he is in the wrong, he is disciplined.'

While United's defence of the 1999-2000 European Cup ended in the quarter-final against the eventual winners Real Madrid – despite a fantastic solo goal by David in the Old Trafford leg – the club won the Premiership again. But what David really yearned for now was to win honours in an England shirt.

'I have won medals with Manchester United at home and in Europe,' he said. 'Now I want to start winning some with an England team that can go all the way at Euro 2000.'

In the run up to the competition, held this time in Belgium and Holland, England had performed creditably in friendlies against Argentina, Brazil and the Ukraine. In contrast to his relationship with previous England boss Glenn Hoddle, David enjoyed working for new national team coach Kevin Keegan, who was also the first to speak of David as a possible future England captain.

But David admitted that he had still not conquered the antipathy felt towards him by some sections of the England supporters, and that troubled him.

It had been made apparent to him during England's 2-0 win over Ukraine at Wembley just before Euro 2000 began. 'We can do really well at Euro 2000 if the fans get behind us all,' he said. 'It never ceases to surprise me some of the stick individual England players get.

'I know there are people in the crowd who actually hate me. That was proved again on Wednesday when I took a throw-in the first half. There were a couple of fans who stood up and absolutely ripped me to shreds.

'I want people on my side because it means so much to me. You are trying hard to do your best for your country and you need to know that people appreciate that.

'There's nothing worse than getting sworn at when you are busting a gut for England. I really thought all that Man U-hating stuff had calmed down a bit. It was just disappointing to realise that it's still around in certain sections.'

Not even that, though, could prepare him for what lay ahead after England's first group match in Euro 2000 against Portugal.

The contest in the Dutch city of Eindhoven had not gone England's way. After a fantastic first 20 minutes they were 2-0 up with goals from Paul Scholes and Steve McManaman. David had been behind both, punishing a defender for standing off him with a pinpoint cross that found the head of his Manchester United team-mate for the first, and then providing the centre from which McManaman thumped England's second.

But the danger signs were already there in Portugal's relaxed and fluid approach work in front of an England goal which too often was left poorly guarded in the rash all-out pursuit of further goals.

Before the match, David had identified his opposite No.7, Luis Figo, as Portugal's principal threat. 'We will have to watch him closely because he can create something out of nothing.'

Figo did precisely that, ghosting through England's

defence to strike an unstoppable drive from fully 30 yards out past Seaman. Eight minutes before half time, slack defending again let in Joao Pinto, who headed home a cross that England failed to block. Nuno Gomes hit the winner for Portugal 15 minutes into the second half.

As the England team trudged disconsolately from the pitch, a small number of spectators unleashed a venomous torrent of abuse in David's direction. In response, a sickened David made a one-fingered gesture in their direction.

That picture was splashed across all the national newspapers the following day. But, with one or two notable exceptions, the general tone of the press coverage of the incident was sympathetic towards David. Kevin Keegan immediately came to his defence.

'If you had heard that abuse, if your sons or daughters had to listen to that, I take my hat off to the players that they didn't react worse,' said Keegan. 'I have had some abuse in my time but that is the worst thing I have seen in football.

'It started at half time and got worse at the end. It was very, very personal. There is a limit to what anybody can take and it got way beyond that. I think David handles himself fantastically well.

'We should talk more about how he handles it, not

what these people are doing to him. There were probably 20,000 England fans there and they were magnificent. We are talking about eight or ten people and I don't understand them.'

David could also rely on Sir Alex Ferguson to support him. 'Nobody in his right mind is going to suggest that Beckham's response to the despicable abuse hurled at him in Eindhoven on Monday night was not regrettable. But any judgement of his conduct should take account of just how horrific the taunts showered on him were,' wrote Ferguson in a newspaper article the weekend after the match.

'Everybody knows that I have not always seen eye to eye with Beckham. The showbiz element in his life, made inevitable by the pop-star status of his wife Victoria, has sometimes caused me to worry about a possible threat to his chances of giving maximum expression to his huge talent.

'But there has never been any doubt that on the field his commitment matches his brilliance, and I admire the way he has coped with pressures no other player in our country has to face.

'He has been guilty of a fair share of follies in his career and, yes, he will have to work harder on self-control. But the cost he has had to pay for his misdemeanours on the pitch has been grossly out of proportion to his wrongdoing.

'That was blatantly true of the petty foul that reduced England to 10 men against Argentina two years ago and is widely (and unconvincingly, in my opinion) held responsible for England's dismissal from the World Cup.

'It was horribly unjust that a moment of stupidity brought him so much suffering. Not many 25-year-olds have been exposed to the public trauma he has had to endure, and my heart went out to him again in Eindhoven, where vile taunts were his reward for being the best player in the England team.'

Victoria also worried about the effect that the abuse had on David. 'It is horrible,' she admitted. 'I get down and depressed just like anybody else. I try not to let it upset me but I am only human. David just has to take it and get on with playing – it is so hard for him.'

England's chances of staying in Euro 2000 were enhanced temporarily in their next match against Germany. For the first time in 34 years, since that July afternoon in 1966 at Wembley when the World Cup was won, England at last defeated their old rivals.

It was not a match to savour. The German team was a mere shadow of the predecessors who in the past three decades had won two World Cups and three European Championships.

But even that did not detract from the vital points that England gained when Alan Shearer stooped to head a curled free-kick from David beyond the German goalkeeper Oliver Kahn.

Briefly, English expectations were raised. But nemesis arrived in the shape once more of Romania. The team who had inflicted an unexpected defeat upon England in the 1998 World Cup repeated the surprise, this time winning 3-2. They went through with the Portuguese to the quarter-finals of the competition.

England had an early opportunity to atone for their Euro 2000 failure, with the qualifying stages of the 2002 World Cup about to begin. Their first opponents were, yet again, Germany.

chapter ELEVEN
captain sensible

October 8 2000 was the day that England said goodbye to Wembley Stadium. What the team hadn't bargained for was that it would also be the day when they said goodbye to their manager, too.

Kevin Keegan's credentials in the job had been called into question ever since England struggled to overcome Scotland 2-1 on aggregate – and were beaten 0-1 at Wembley – in the play-offs for Euro 2000. Then came the early exit from the competition itself during which Keegan's tactics, or apparent lack of them, attracted heavy criticism.

The disquiet about the manager's strategy finally reached the England squad itself in the build-up to their opening qualifier for the 2002 World Cup against Germany.

The players should have fancied their chances after

the long-awaited defeat of the Germans at Euro 2000. Instead some players spoke out for the first time, disagreeing with Keegan's decision to play defender Gareth Southgate out of position in midfield for such an important match. Their concern would be shown to be justified.

Certainly England never looked at ease on a drizzly afternoon that matched the gloom felt over the performance. A free kick from Liverpool's Dietmar Hamann from a full 35 yards out after only 13 minutes beat a defensive wall that was not even in position when the kick was taken, and a late-diving David Seaman.

David's face as he was substituted eight minutes from the end, and the derisive boos and whistles of the England fans once it was over, told their own story. His own free kicks had not pierced the German defence, goalkeeper Oliver Kahn safely smothering the first one and then making a fine save from Tony Adams' header from the second.

The abuse that rained down on Keegan as he retreated to the tunnel made up his mind. After informing the players that this was as far as he went with the England team, he then left the dressing room to make the same announcement on live television.

David was genuinely upset for Keegan. 'I will never

say a bad word about Kevin Keegan. I rang him about two months after he resigned as England coach just to say hello and to see how he was. He had been in a similar position to me, dealing with the pressures of celebrity, and he went out of his way to help me through those problems.'

As the Football Association cast around for a successor, England's misery was compounded by a mediocre 0-0 draw in Finland under the caretaker-management of Under-21 coach Howard Wilkinson. Even at this early stage, the next World Cup looked out of reach.

The FA eventually caused a storm by breaking with precedent and appointing a foreign-born England coach for the first time in its history. Sven-Goran Eriksson was one of the most respected coaches in Europe, having won trophies with IFK Gothenburg in his native Sweden, Benfica of Portugal, and latterly in Italy, with Sampdoria and then Lazio, whom he'd led the previous season to their first championship in quarter of a century.

Eriksson's contract with Lazio stipulated that he stay with the club until the end of the Italian season. So in the meantime the FA put Peter Taylor in temporary charge of the England team.

Taylor, by now manager of Leicester City, had

established his reputation as the coach of the England Under-21 team, which remained unbeaten under his control. Taylor's first game in charge – and as it would turn out, his only one – was a friendly against Italy in Turin. He decided to rely on the sort of young players who had been instrumental to his success with the Under-21s and he had already made up his mind whom he wanted as his captain.

'My phone rang at 8am. I had only just woken up with Brooklyn,' David would later recall. 'We were staying at Gary Neville's house because Victoria was in London, where she had been working in the recording studio.

'I was still half asleep and my immediate thought was: "Who on earth can be calling at this time of the morning?"

'I was surprised to discover that it was Peter Taylor on the end of the line. The news he had for me was even more staggering.

'He told me: "I have decided to make you captain of England. I wanted to let you know first before the news breaks." It was unbelievable, something everyone who has ever pulled on a pair of football boots dreams about.

'To be captain of my country...words cannot describe my feelings. It is the biggest honour a

'I immediately rang Victoria and then told the rest of the family. They were just as thrilled and speechless as I was.'

Given what had happened only two years earlier against Argentina, and the reaction that had followed, Taylor's decision could be regarded as either brave or reckless. But he entertained no doubts.

'I thought of how controlled David had been after the World Cup sending off, and despite all the foul abuse and even personal threats heaped on him for apparently being responsible for us losing,' he said.

'No sportsman has ever had to contend with anything so bad and so unfair, and yet he came through it with dignity and held himself high.'

One of David's first thoughts was for Tony Adams, the retiring England captain, and the man who had been the first to comfort him after the Argentina sending off.

'Tony was great to me after what happened at the World Cup and two years on it's astonishing that I'm captain of England,' he admitted.

'I'll never forget what Tony did for me – I needed it at the time – and maybe in the future, if I'm still captain, other players might need the same kind of comforting that he gave me.

'Two years ago, I wasn't very popular with a lot of people – and now I'm leading out the England team. For me, that's the most special thing that could happen.'

He admitted that he might not seem an obvious candidate as captain, and not just because he had only ever done it twice before, once with United's youth team, and then in the second half of a Premiership match after Roy Keane went off injured.

There was the suspicion that he might not be a forceful enough personality to impose himself upon a team as its leader. But as he pointed out on the eve of the Italy match: 'The biggest influence I can give to players is what I can do with my feet, not my mouth.'

One of the reasons why Taylor chose David as his captain was witnessed by a journalist watching England in training on the Turin pitch the day before the match: after the rest of the squad were back in the showers, the new captain was still out there on his own, practising free kicks.

On the night, England lost 0-1, but their young side impressed supporters and neutral observers alike – not least the captain, especially when he refused to react after being struck by an opponent. 'I was impressed with every aspect of David's captaincy,' said Taylor after the match. 'I didn't want him ranting and raving. Instead he did some wonderful things.'

Not long after the match against Italy, Sven-Goran Eriksson completed his appointment as England coach, after he was released from his contract by Lazio. Unlike some critics, who regarded his arrival as some sort of insult to the English game, David welcomed Eriksson.

'A lot of people wanted an Englishman as manager but I don't have a problem with him being Swedish. He has worked with some big clubs and some great players and been very successful. He deserves all our support.'

What he still didn't know was whether or not Eriksson would keep him as captain, even though the new England coach had already paid him a glowing tribute in his new book, *Inside Football – The Mental Game.*

'Some players manage to maintain a very high physical tempo, but even so they also maintain an inner calm in difficult situations on the pitch,' wrote Eriksson.'This gives them an overview, time to evaluate the situation, as well as technical control.

'Some sportsmen have natural ability in this area. In football it is enough to mention names like Pele, Zidane, Figo and Beckham.'

Franz Beckenbauer, too, weighed in with fulsome

praise. The man who had won the World Cup as both a captain and a manager with Germany, claimed: 'David Beckham is simply the most exciting, talented footballer in the world.'

On the day before England's first match under Eriksson, a friendly against Spain at Villa Park, the new coach informed David that he would be keeping the captain's armband. 'He just told me in the team hotel before the match against Spain that it had been mine before he came and I deserved to keep it.'

England got off to winning ways under Eriksson, defeating Spain 3-0, and it stayed that way. In his first World Cup qualifier in charge, England beat Finland 2-1 at Anfield, and two unusual things happened to David: he scored for his country for only the second time the winning goal, three years after his free kick against Colombia in the World Cup – and he also had the highly unusual experience of hearing 'there's only one David Beckham' chanted at the home of one of United's biggest rivals.

He scored again in the next qualifying group victory, 2-0 against Greece in Athens. This time it was his speciality – a curling 25-yard free-kick – and that despite being hit by objects, including coins, hurled by the crowd. 'He behaved like a captain. He is scoring goals and playing great football,' said Eriksson.

David felt the captaincy had improved his game. 'I feel more liberated as captain and I think I'm playing with more freedom.' This was the role he had always dreamed of having for United and England – a more central one which did not just restrict him to the right flank.

'Everything has clicked since I became captain and I thrive on the responsibility. Having players like Paul Scholes and Steven Gerrard in midfield has also helped. When you have players like that who can win the ball and pass it around well, it creates more chances.'

A 3-1 win in Albania followed, as England's momentum under its new manager continued. The players were equally pleased with their new captain. 'There are several reasons why he is perfect for the job,' said Phil Neville. 'One is his age. I think we need a captain now who is going to be skipper for the next five, six or maybe 10 years.

'In the first game against Italy he certainly led by example but you sense now he's getting more and more comfortable and confident with the other players.

'He does have an aura about him. When he walks into the room you sense the young players – and some of the older ones, too – would do anything for him. When he talks, they listen and that is a great asset for a captain.'

Paul Scholes agreed. 'People always seem to think you need a skipper who is always shouting. David is not like that and he has not tried to change. He leads more by example than anything.'

David himself recognised what having Eriksson in charge had brought to the England team. 'Probably the best quality we have learned under our new coach is to be patient and stick to our good habits, even when we are going through a bad spell.

'If there is one thing Sven has stressed, it is that we must not just hit balls over the top of the opposition and then try to get it back. There are times, especially when you have players as fast as Michael Owen, when the direct ball can work, but most of the play has to be crisp passes with a compact team.'

Never was that strategy, or the speed of Owen, to be put to better effect than on an unforgettable night in Munich on September 1 2001.

Yet in the days leading up to England's crucial qualifier against Germany, David's place in the team was in doubt, after he limped off the pitch in United's Premiership match at Aston Villa.

An intensive week of massage and physiotherapy healed the groin strain he had suffered. David's aim now was to make up for the pain of the final match at Wembley 11 months previously.

'The way we felt is what we want to make the Germans feel tomorrow,' he said on the eve of the tie. 'We were so disappointed, not just because it was the Germans but also the last game at Wembley.'

The historic task of the scale facing England could hardly be over-estimated. The national side had never before won a competitive fixture on German soil. Even more awesomely, Germany had lost only once previously in 61 World Cup qualifying matches at home, and that was to Portugal in 1985 after they had already gone through to the finals.

When their striker Carsten Jancker seized on a defensive lapse to put Germany a goal up after only six minutes, England fans could not help but worry that history was about to repeat itself yet again. But instead it was England who took the initiative, and levelled the scoreline six minutes later.

David's free kick had looked overhit, but Steven Gerrard retrieved the ball before it ran out of play and looped the ball towards Gary Neville. He headed goalward, Nick Barmby nipped in to reach the ball before German goalkeeper Oliver Kahn, and nodded it into the path of Michael Owen who smashed it into the net.

While the Germans proceeded to miss an open goal and then force a brilliant stop from David Seaman,

England got the priceless advantage of a goal just before half-time.

Once more, it originated from a less than impressive free kick from David, but the German defence only half cleared it. The ball went as far as Gerrard, who cracked in an unstoppable drive beyond the reach of Kahn.

Three minutes after the restart, England were 3-1 up, when the Germans' chief tormentor, Owen, finished with a clinical flick from Emile Heskey's headed pass, after David had crossed.

If it was Owen getting the goals, it was the captain who was controlling the match, prompting nearly every England move. After Owen had completed his first hat-trick for England from a through pass by Gerrard, David then combined with Paul Scholes to put through Heskey for a fifth.

England had won perhaps the most amazing international victory in their history. So it was not surprising that, when offered the chance to come off before the end, David refused.

Thinking of the muscle strain that had nearly ruled him out of the match altogether, the England bench signalled for him to come off with 15 minutes remaining. They had no chance of succeeding.

'They wanted to bring me off a few times towards

the end but I said: "No." Who would want to miss out on a finish like that?

'I'm absolutely loving the responsibility of being captain, especially in a team like this one. You're still proud even when you're not getting results but to get them from playing football like the way we did against Germany is extra special.'

The players had no doubt of the debt they owed the captain. Stephen Gerrard said: 'I admire David as a captain and he's the best player we've got – the key man. We all look up to him and respect him as the captain. He leads by example and always puts in a good performance. All the lads love him.'

They would soon have even more reason to do so.

chapter TWELVE
saviour

What do you see when you think of David Beckham?

For many people it is one half of the most talked and written about couple in the country.

The popular simplistic image portrayed of David and Victoria is one that the couple themselves regard with an amused detachment. '"Posh'n'Becks" – yeeuck!' said Victoria once. 'We always say: "Those two, they're so annoying." We look at them from the outside and think: "Well, he's a prat, he doesn't have a brain. She bosses him around, he's just some pretty boy. And Posh – miserable bossy old cow." It makes us laugh.'

No other footballer could command front page headlines simply by having a haircut. David shaved off the Mohican he had had done in the summer of 2001 within weeks, because he didn't want to be held responsible for children getting into trouble at school for imitating the style, as was being reported.

There's a fascination about his tattoos, his cars, and virtually every item of clothing he wears off the football pitch. He is paid huge sums to model designer sunglasses because the makers know his name sells.

At the University of Staffordshire in Stoke-on-Trent there is a degree course in David Beckham Studies. At the Pariwas Buddhist temple in Thailand, a gold-plated statue has been sculpted in his image – his old one, that is, when he had longer hair.

When Manchester United went on a tour of the Far East before the start of the 2001-02 season, the squad was nearly crushed by frenzied mobs desperate to greet all the players – but one of them in particular. No pop idol could have had a more hysterical welcome.

But while all that is undoubtedly part of the David Beckham phenomenon, they are all merely sideshows, distractions from the substance.

The real David Beckham can be found in the person who had to survive the unprecedented coverage that followed his return from that sending off in the 1998 World Cup.

One journalist put it like this. 'Can you imagine conducting *your* career with 60 million people watching your every mistake worldwide? Imagine if *you* got back from an international trip and people were burning your effigy all over the country because they hated you.

'Imagine thousands of people screaming abuse and profanity at you every time you went into the office. Imagine them insulting your wife in as many deeply personal ways as they could think of and then singing about it as loud as they could all around you.

'And yet, somehow, in the midst of this raw, aggressive competition, still in his young and angry 20s, he manages – for the most part – not to freak out.'

The real David Beckham is the one that Sir Alex Ferguson has known since the frail-looking boy from East London first went to Manchester United.

'David Beckham is Britain's finest striker of a football,' declared the United manager, 'not because of God-given talent but because he practises with a relentless application that the vast majority of less gifted players wouldn't contemplate.

'He may look as if butter wouldn't melt in his mouth. But underneath the boyish appearance and all the trappings of trendiness there is a steely determination.'

And all those gifts would be condensed into one glorious, career-defining moment in the dying seconds of a match that seemed destined to condemn England to World Cup failure and render meaningless the exploits of that 5-1 victory over Germany.

After the triumph of Munich, England had overcome a nervy start to eventually beat Albania 2-0 in their next group match, with goals from Michael Owen and Robbie Fowler.

In the final contests of European qualifying Group Nine, England faced Greece at Old Trafford with a superior goal difference to second-placed Germany, who faced Finland, also that afternoon.

It was a match England was overwhelmingly expected to win. Instead, early nerves had turned into growing panic as first Greece took the lead in the first half, then substitute Teddy Sheringham equalised from a free kick by David in the second, only for Greece to go back in front within a minute.

The unthinkable was unfolding in front of the horrified England supporters. Greece, a team that had struggled to score against England in their previous international meetings, let alone ever beat them, was on the verge of victory.

Throughout the increasingly desperate proceedings, David had stood head and shoulders above his strangely uninspired team-mates, tackling and passing, cajoling and prompting, and running, always running.

But, when he needed it most, his free kick skill

seemed to have deserted him. He had aimed seven of them at the Greek goal during the match. They had gone over the bar, wide of a post, been saved by the goalkeeper or struck the side-netting.

On the bench, Sven-Goran Eriksson was kept in constant touch with the score in Gelsenkirchen, where Germany and Finland had kicked off slightly before England.

As the final whistle blew in the German match to conclude a 0-0 draw, Eriksson signalled the result to his players by making his thumb and forefinger on either hand into the shape of two noughts.

By now, the scoreline from Gelsenkirchen had flashed around the Old Trafford crowd too, increasing the air of tension. Unless England could score, Germany would win the automatic qualification spot from the group to the World Cup.

The German players coming off the pitch after their match, now crowded around a television monitor on the touchline to watch the last moments of England's match, confident they had done enough to go through.

Nigel Martyn, standing in for the injured David Seaman in England's goal, launched the ball upfield for one final assault in the 92nd minute. The ball dropped towards Teddy Sheringham, who fell under a challenge from a Greek defender. Fortunately for England, the referee awarded a free kick.

Just before David placed the ball, Teddy Sheringham walked up and offered to take the kick. 'I felt it might be a good idea for me to take one just to break it up, to let the keeper think about what was going on,' he said. 'But he kept on saying: "It's a good area for me."'

Sheringham had also offered to take the previous free kick that David had taken. 'The first time I said: "No, this one's going in," and the second one I said: "No, this one's too far for you." He just laughed and let me take them.'

Now, as David prepared to take what would surely be his last free kick of the match, Gary Neville called over: 'You need to score this one.'

In Gelsenkirchen, some German fans were already celebrating, thinking that the England game was over. Eriksson, watching from the touchline, would say after the match: 'There is nobody else in world football I'd rather have taking a free kick in that situation.'

What crossed his mind as he ran up to strike the ball? The long evenings in Chase Lane park near his childhood home, trying to stay out playing football for as long as he could before having to go home?

His dad's, and later Alex Ferguson's repeated urgings to practise, practise, practise? Going out on the training ground with a bag of balls to take shot after shot at an empty goal to perfect the technique?

Or maybe the never-forgotten advice of Eric Harrison, the youth team coach at Old Trafford who had first moulded his talent, to 'play the game and not the occasion'?

The ball left his foot and lifted over the wall of Greek defenders, swerving all the time, struck with such pace that the goalkeeper never got near it, and with such precision that it arrowed unerringly into the top corner of the net.

England 2 - Greece 2.

Seconds later, as the final whistle blew, David was engulfed by relieved team-mates. On the lap of honour around Old Trafford afterwards, most of them at least had the humility to look a little sheepish. All of them were aware that their own largely uninspiring performances had been rescued by his one supreme moment.

In that moment, David Beckham had more than repaid the 'supposed' debt that he owed the country – the perception that his rashness had been the reason for England's downfall in the 1998 World Cup.

Instead, with that final dramatic free kick, he had secured the 2-2 draw with Greece which guaranteed that England would be playing in Japan and South Korea in 2002. And in doing so he had become the saviour of England and a hero for the nation.

That was the real David Beckham.